Empower, Don't Overpower

Modern Management Strategies for High-Trust Leadership

OrangeBooks Publication

1st Floor, Rajhans Arcade, Mall Road, Kohka, Bhilai, Chhattisgarh 490020

Website: **www.orangebooks.in**

First Edition, 2025

ISBN: 978-93-6554-295-0

Price: Rs. 350.00

Printed in India

EMPOWER DON'T OVERPOWER

Modern Management Strategies For High-Trust Leadership

DR. BALVINDER SINGH BANGA

OrangeBooks Publication
www.orangebooks.in

Disclaimer

This book is based on real events, personal experiences, and professional insights. However, to protect the privacy and identities of individuals and organizations, **some names, roles, locations, and company details have been changed or fictionalized**. Any resemblance to actual individuals, living or deceased, or to actual organisations is **purely coincidental and unintentional**, unless explicitly stated.

The content is intended to inform, inspire, and provoke thoughtful reflection.

Dedication

To the **woman I walk life with Ritu**, whose strength softens my storms and whose silence speaks the loudest support.

To the **woman whose memory fuels my values my beloved mother**, gone from sight but never from soul, still whispering wisdom two decades later.

To the **boys who make every tomorrow worth striving for Mansidak and Kohinoor**, may you grow to lead not with power, but with purpose and compassion.

To every **team member and colleague**, from high-rise MNC boardrooms to passionate promoter-led floors wherever I worked, I walked among over 150 minds at a time. Each team, each challenge, and each breakthrough built this book.

You didn't just work with me you helped me understand what it truly means to lead.

"Leadership isn't about being in charge. It's about caring enough to let others rise."

- Dr. Balvinder S. Banga

Acknowledgements

Writing this book has been a journey of reflection, growth, and gratitude, and it would not have been possible without the unwavering support of those who've walked beside me.

To **Ritu**, my wife, your strength and quiet encouragement have been my anchor. Thank you for believing in me, even when I questioned myself.

To my late mother, **Lt. Satinder Pall Kaur,** though you left this world over two decades ago, your values and love continue to guide every step I take.

To **Mansidak and Kohinoor**, my sons, your curiosity and evolving worldviews push me to keep growing. You are my greatest teachers and my proudest legacy.

To every organization and colleague I've worked with, from global corporations to agile, promoter-led enterprises, thank you for shaping my understanding of leadership. Across every company,

I've had the privilege of learning from over **500+ talented individuals**. This book reflects not just my journey, but ours.

To the mentors, peers, and friends who lent their wisdom and trust your influence runs through these pages.

And to you, the reader thanks you for choosing a path of empowerment. I hope this book serves you as a companion in your own leadership journey.

- Dr. Balvinder S. Banga

✨ The Spirit of This Book

ਮਿਠਤੁ ਨੀਵੀ ਨਾਨਕਾ ਗੁਣ ਚੰਗਿਆਈਆ ਤਤੁ ॥

"Sweetness and humility, O Nanak,
are the essence of virtue and goodness."
— Sri Guru Granth Sahib Ji, Ang 470

This book is the result of the belief that ***leadership is not domination but service, empathy, and dignity***.

In an age obsessed with power and speed, "Empower, Don't Overpower" is a reminder that the humblest are often the most powerful leaders.

Drawing from **Gurbani**, modern psychology, and real-world experiences, this book blends **timeless wisdom with today's leadership needs**. Whether you're guiding teams, raising children, teaching students, or influencing communities this book offers a path built on.

- High-trust leadership
- Emotional intelligence
- Courage without aggression
- And power that uplifts, not controls

Inspired by the lives of **Guru Nanak Dev Ji** and **Guru Gobind Singh Ji**, this book reflects a leadership philosophy rooted in **Seva (selfless service), Sabhar (patience), and Sach (truth).**

Let this book be your **companion in creating spaces where others feel safe to rise.**

Not by your command, but because of your trust.

Let us begin not with power, but with **sweetness and humility**.

Contents

Introduction

In an era defined by rapid technological disruption, shifting workplace dynamics, and evolving societal expectations, the way we understand leadership is undergoing a seismic transformation. No longer is leadership about commanding from the top; it is about connecting, guiding, and empowering those around us. Empower, Don't Overpower is both a response to and a blueprint for this new reality.

Across the globe, organizations are awakening to the realization that the old models rooted in hierarchy, compliance, and fear are no longer sustainable. These traditional structures, while once effective, now stifle creativity, limit collaboration, and undermine trust. In their place, a new model is emerging, one that places empathy over ego, shared vision over individual dominance, and empowerment over authority. This book is a manifesto for that model.

Drawing on evidence-based research, real-world leadership practices, and personal experience, Empower, Don't Overpower explores what it truly means to lead with purpose and humanity. It invites leaders of all types—not just CEOs or managers, but also teachers, parents, coaches, and community advocates—to rethink their roles as facilitators of growth, not gatekeepers of power.

Each chapter is designed to build on the last, creating a cumulative learning experience that delves into diverse contexts.

- From empowering teams and workplaces to nurturing resilience in children.
- From creating inclusive educational environments to using technology as a tool for equitable access.
- From building cultural and community bridges to shaping policy grounded in justice and empathy.

The heart of this book lies in **high-trust leadership**—a philosophy that insists leadership is not about control but about cultivating confidence, autonomy, and mutual respect. It advocates for emotional intelligence, active listening, transparency, and the courage to let others shine. In doing so, it shows that empowered people are more innovative, more committed, and more capable of achieving lasting impact.

This book isn't just theory—it's actionable. The tools, frameworks, and case studies from various sectors equip readers to lead not just effectively, but ethically. Whether you're leading a team in a startup, mentoring students in a classroom, or guiding your family through challenges, these principles apply.

Most importantly, *Empower, Don't Overpower* is a call to embrace a different kind of power—the kind ***that lifts others, builds trust, and reshapes the future***.

Let this book be your guide as you lead with intention, influence with integrity, and empower others to reach their fullest potential.

"Empowerment is not just giving tasks—it's about fostering belief, providing tools, and trusting people to grow."

Dr. Balvinder S. Banga

Chapter - 1
Understanding Empowerment

What Empowerment Is?

Empowerment is a multifaceted concept that is at the heart of leadership and individual growth. It is essentially about giving individuals or groups the resources, tools, and authority to take charge of their lives and make choices that will determine their destiny. This is a concept that transcends the mere delegation of work; it is a deeper articulation of trust, respect, and cooperation that sets the tone where people feel respected and empowered.

The empowerment ethos is the merging of support and autonomy. Empowerment calls for a move away from conventional hierarchical structures to an inclusive and participative one. In an empowered setting, people are inspired to make their opinions heard, to offer ideas, and to be accountable. Not only does this participative process contribute to people's individual development, but it also strengthens the group's or organization's collective power.

The most critical element of empowerment is establishing self-efficacy, that is, people feeling that they are capable of doing something. When people are empowered, they will challenge themselves, stay motivated in the face of challenges, and achieve their goals. This sense of self-efficacy tends to be established as a result of being offered the proper training, proper equipment, and chances for personal as well as professional development.

Empowerment also comes with the concept of accountability. When individuals are empowered, they will be held accountable for the decisions and actions they take. Such accountability begets responsibility and commitment, and this could lead to improved performance and productivity. Moreover, when individuals are held accountable, they are likely to learn and keep on improving, thereby increasing their competencies and skills.

***Empowerment, in the context of leadership, is the act of creating an environment in which the feeling of being valued and respected by team members is enabled*.** Empowering leaders are able to spot positive strengths in people and use them to propel collective goals. Empowering leaders lead and advise but give team members the freedom of learning and innovating. Empowering leadership not only boosts morale but also triggers creativity and innovation, and the organization becomes stronger and more dynamic.

The benefits of empowerment do not end at organizational and individual development. Empowerment also has significant implications for social and economic development. Empowered individuals are more likely to participate actively in their communities, advocate for change, and contribute to the overall well-being of society. This ripple effect can result in more equitable and sustainable development outcomes, particularly in marginalized or disadvantaged groups.

However, empowerment is not without its challenges. It requires a cultural shift and a reversal of existing power dynamics. Resistance to change, fear of loss of control, and lack of trust can hinder the empowerment process. Therefore, it is essential to foster an environment of openness and transparency, where communication is encouraged and feedback is valued. By addressing these challenges, organizations and communities can create a more inclusive and empowering environment for all.

In summary, empowerment is a dynamic and transformative process that enables individuals and groups to realize their full potential. ***It is a powerful tool for fostering personal growth, enhancing organizational effectiveness, and driving social change***. By understanding and embracing the principles of empowerment, we can create a more equitable and sustainable future for everyone.

Historical Context

The history of empowerment, particularly in organizational and social contexts, has been shaped by a complex tapestry of historical events, ideologies, and movements. In its beginnings, there is a profound intertwining of power relations and the desire for agency and autonomy.

Empowerment traces its roots back to the Enlightenment era, when there emerged new philosophical ideas revolving around the application of the individual's reason and the use of human potential for betterment. John Locke and Jean-Jacques Rousseau challenged the power structure in place, maintaining the natural rights and freedom of human beings. This philosophy served as the basis for the establishment of democratic principles, which would later be utilized as a source of inspiration for most empowerment initiatives.

Guru Nanak Dev Ji, the founder of Sikhism, in 15th century also **challenged traditional power structures**—both **religious** and **political** but did so from a deeply **spiritual and social** perspective. He spoke against the injustices of rulers like Babar, calling out **oppression, tyranny, and abuse of power** in his verses. Like Rousseau and Locke, he believed that no one had a divine right to rule over others unjustly.

As the 19th century unfolded, the Industrial Revolution brought about significant economic and social changes. The shift from agrarian economies to industrialized societies led to the rise of the working class and, consequently, new forms of labor organization. Empowerment during this period was often manifested through labor movements and unions, which sought to improve conditions for workers and assert their rights in the face of burgeoning industrial capitalists. These movements highlighted the need for collective action as a means to achieve empowerment and challenge oppressive systems.

The 20th century witnessed further expansion of empowerment concepts, particularly through the lens of social justice movements. The civil rights movement in the United States, the struggle against apartheid in South

Africa, and the global women's rights movement are just a few examples of collective efforts to dismantle systemic inequalities and promote empowerment for marginalized groups. These movements underscored the importance of structural change and policy reform as avenues to facilitate empowerment. In India, the independence movement led by Mahatma Gandhi not only sought political freedom but also championed **social empowerment** through non-violence, self- reliance, and the up-liftment of the oppressed, including Dalits and women. Post-independence, movements such as the Dalit assertion led by Dr. B.R. Ambedkar, women's rights campaigns, and grassroots mobilizations for land and labor reforms further emphasized the need for structural change and policy reform. These global and national efforts underscored that true empowerment requires transforming unjust systems and ensuring equal access to rights, opportunities, and dignity for all.

organizational forms to more open and participative forms of organization was a reflection of growing recognition that employee empowerment had benefits. Managerial theories such as employee participation, participative decision-making, and flat organizations became more significant as it was shown through evidence that empowered workers were more innovative, productive, and fulfilled.

In recent decades, the revolution of the digital age has also reshaped the empowerment landscape. Diffusion of the internet and digital technologies has placed information in the hands of ever more people, enabling them to communicate, share, and organize on an unprecedented level. Social networking sites, in particular, have proved themselves to be powerful tools for campaigning and activism, empowering the voiceless and enabling the instant propagation of ideas.

Today, though, the debate about empowerment is a fluid one, informed by new world challenges such as climate change, economic inequity, and political instability. As nations grapple with these complex issues, empowerment—both collective and individual—continues to be an imperative that is needed. A consideration of the history of empowerment leads us to the ongoing quest for equilibrium between power and agency, and to the ongoing imperative to design spaces that empower and not overpower individuals and groups.

Empowerment vs. Control

In leadership and management, it is the balance between control and empowerment that makes an organization succeed or fail. Empowerment refers to the freedom, resources, and support provided to individuals to make decisions and take initiatives. Control is seen when there is close observation, strict rules, and centralized decision-making.

The power of empowerment is that it establishes a culture that promotes innovation and creativity. When individuals are free to try and apply their solutions, they will be more likely to own and be committed to their work. Not only does this improve morale, it improves productivity, too, because employees feel more willing to contribute when they believe their contribution counts.

Empowerment also builds a culture of trust. Empowering leaders trust their people, and this makes team members also trust their judgment and abilities. This can lead to improved communication and collaboration among teams because individuals feel that they are able to express themselves and their opinions without their being criticized.

But on the other hand, a control-based managerial style can also suppress creativity and innovation. Excessive management of employees can actually make them overly reliant on managerial guidance, inhibiting their own capacity to think and resolve issues independently. This can lead to demotivation and lower job satisfaction, as employees feel underappreciated and stifled by a system that will not permit them to achieve their best.

Secondly, excessive control gives rise to the bottleneck effect whereby decisions are taken at the center and are time-consuming. This makes an organization slow to respond to change or problems because all decisions have to pass through a series of approvals. In a fast-paced business environment, rapid response is extremely crucial, and empowerment makes organizations responsive and quick to respond.

But what needs to be emphasized is that empowerment is not the absence of structure or direction. There needs to be a balance where individuals are granted the leeway to innovate within a structure that aligns with the goals and values of the organization. There needs to be clear expectations, resources, and support so that empowerment will not result in chaos.

And not all will thrive under an empowered system. There will be some who require a little more guidance and structure in order to thrive. It is the job of quality leadership to recognize such differences and adapt their style to suit, offering a balance between empowerment and control that is appropriate to person and team needs.

Last but not least, the shift from control to empowerment reflects a better understanding of human motivation and organizational dynamics. With increased emphasis on sustainable development and employee satisfaction, the empowerment model is not only a strategic choice, but also a necessity. It builds a people-centered culture of people willing to perform to the best, as well as a climate of continuous improvement and innovation. This, in turn, prompts organizations to achieve their objectives more efficiently and effectively.

What is empowerment when a company moves from command-and-control in the actual world? Surya Textiles' tale offers an exciting insight

📘 Case Story: "The Shift at Surya Textiles"

Down in Ludhiana's industrial belt, Surya Textiles had been operated on a conventional top-down basis for years. Workers took orders, overseers enforced compliance, and innovation was the exception. Turnover was high, and morale was low.

And then, in 2020, Priya, a diverse leadership-trained young leader, was appointed as the new head of plant. Her first action **was not to command, but to listen**.

She held roundtable meetings with the floor staff, introduced a "suggestion box" that was acted upon, and held training sessions wherein machine operators learned basic finance, safety, and problem-solving.

One of her most significant adjustments was delegating small group leadership responsibilities to seasoned staff members. Each group was assigned its own quality checks and small scheduling to handle. The outcome? Productivity jumped **23% in six months**, and employee satisfaction scores almost doubled.

The actual breakthrough was obtained when floor worker Nitin suggested a redesign of the layout that decreased waste travel time by 30%.

Under the old system, his idea would've never left his lips. Under the new system, it became policy.

Surya Textiles left process behind—it transformed individuals. **Empowerment did not maximize performance it gave meaning.**

As this transformation indicates, empowerment not only unleashes productivity and creativity but human energy to lead, contribute, and grow. Let us now observe the broader benefits organizations can reap by making empowerment a practical reality.

Benefits of Empowerment

Empowerment is an impetus for growth, creating a vibrant atmosphere in which people and organizations can excel. Empowerment is essentially giving individuals autonomy, tools, and confidence to allow them to make decisions, resolve problems, and act. This activity not only fosters individual growth but also organizational achievement.

One of the biggest strengths of empowerment is higher worker motivation and engagement. Empowering workers makes them more responsible and answerable for their jobs and work, which results in greater job satisfaction. This sense of responsibility results in a more committed and active workforce as workers feel that their work is worth it and contributing. Empowerment as a process enables creativity and innovation through the ability to experiment with new ideas with the ability to fail without any reprisal. This culture of trust and support enables workers to be innovative, and this results in new solutions and process and product improvements.

Furthermore, empowerment significantly contributes to improved decision-making ability. Empowered individuals are encouraged to make decisions themselves and utilize their experience, leading to quicker and smarter decisions. Decentralization of decision-making not only improves the effectiveness of the organization but also allows quicker response to issues and opportunities. Empowered organizations have few bottlenecks, since decisions will not go through many levels of hierarchy before action is taken.

Empowerment is also vital in creating a culture of responsibility and accountability. When employees are given a lot of responsibility, they become more accountable for their performance and results. Responsibility puts pressure on individuals to perform better and push for change in the areas that are not doing well. The responsible culture that is created encourages a problem-solving culture where employees anticipate problems and solve them before they become problems.

The benefits of empowerment extend beyond organizational performance and individual growth. Empowered employees are more likely to be committed and dedicated to their organization, resulting in less turnover and associated costs. As organizations invest in their human capital, they establish a sense of belonging and loyalty that translates into lower recruitment and training expenses.

Furthermore, empowerment generates diversity and inclusion in the workplace. Through the embracing and execution of diverse ideas, businesses are capable of accessing a larger reservoir of ideas and expertise, and are thus more innovative and responsive. Empowerment results in individuals from diverse backgrounds providing ideas, and thus a more inclusive and collective work environment.

Empowerment, when used in a leadership context, is the opposite of the traditional dynamic between leaders and groups. Empowering leaders are facilitators and coaches and not directive leaders, leading and guiding but not leading. It opens the door to greater communication and trust, building more cohesive and better-performing teams.

In general, empowerment has many advantages that have long-lasting consequences. By providing a context where individuals feel comfortable to initiate, innovate, and be held responsible, companies are able to release the full potential of their workforce. Not only does this drive individual and company growth, but it also puts companies in a position to thrive in the future in a fast-evolving context.

The Psychology of Empowerment

"When people believe in their own ability to succeed, they stop waiting for permission to act."

— Dr. Balvinder S. Banga

Chapter - 2
The Psychology of Empowerment

Self-Efficacy

It is in the quest for personal empowerment that one must learn about the concept of self-efficacy. It is the belief of an individual that he or she is capable of performing actions necessary to accomplish something. It is not merely possessing the skills but also believing in applying the skills to accomplish something. Self-efficacy has a huge impact on people's thoughts, behaviors, and emotions.

The importance of self-efficacy is that it has extreme power in terms of affecting motivation and persistence. Those with high self-efficacy are going to have higher goals for themselves, take greater control over their activities, and display hardness during difficult circumstances. They will be more likely to perceive challenging tasks as a means of acquiring knowledge and not as impossible hurdles. This frame of mind creates a mastery strategy of professional and personal development, where setbacks are temporary and overcome.

Conversely, those with low self-efficacy feel helpless and unclear. They avoid challenging tasks because they fear criticism, rejection, and failure. This creates a stagnating effect, as potential development and growth will be avoided. It is necessary to operationalize this construct in order to develop environments that will empower and not inadvertently overpower the individual by setting unrealistic standards or too much control.

Developing self-efficacy involves a number of key strategies. One effective strategy is through mastery experiences. The ability to perform tasks increases confidence and reinforces the sense of capability. Successes, regardless of their size, can actually increase self-efficacy, providing a foundation for the success of more demanding challenges.

Social modeling is also an important part. Witnessing others, especially those that one is paired with, accomplish things allows for increased trust in oneself. Vicarious experience provides the sense of potential, and it encourages individuals to attempt similar activities.

Verbal persuasion is also employed in maintaining self-efficacy. Positive reinforcement and encouragement by leaders, colleagues, and mentors can reinforce a person's belief in his or her ability. It is important, however, that this reinforcement is realistic and specific, highlighting the strengths of the individual and the aspects wherein he or she should be improved.

Emotional and physical states can play a dramatic role in influencing self-efficacy. Tension, stress, and fatigue can drain confidence, while serenity and energy can construct it. Regulation of emotion and experiencing a state of mind balance is all part of the process of sustaining a confident sense of self-efficacy.

Self-efficacy is not static, but it is varied with experience and learning. Through the establishment of mastery-oriented environments, positive models, and constructive feedback, individuals are able to develop a healthy self-efficacy. Through empowerment, they can manage the challenges of life confidently and resiliently, thus having a more successful and fulfilling life.

In the broad context of empowerment, the establishment self-efficacy is not simply interested in personal development.

It aids in the overall growth of societies, organizations, and communities. Empowered individuals become productive within their environment, encouraging innovation, collaboration, and progress. Therefore, possession of knowledge and the development of self-efficacy is the platform of empowerment, and it enables individuals not only to survive but thrive in a changing world. Through the emphasis on self-efficacy, we build the platform for lifelong learning and adaptive success, whereby every challenge is a lesson and a chance to grow.

The effect of self-efficacy becomes increasingly real when seen within everyday life. Aarav's story is a testimony to the fact that belief in oneself—when fostered can lead to change-oriented development. growth.

📘 Story: "Aarav's Awakening"

At a bustling tech company in Hyderabad, **Aarav**, a mid-level engineer, had begun to feel stuck. Brilliant but quiet, he rarely poke up in meetings and often second-guessed his skills. His manager, noticing this, enrolled him in a **mentorship program** focused on **self-efficacy and autonomy**.

The first step was small—Aarav was asked to **lead a sprint meeting**. His voice trembled at first, but he prepared meticulously. By the third session, team members began to seek his input proactively. That single experience sparked a change.

With **consistent encouragement, peer support, and room to fail**, Aarav slowly grew into a confident contributor. He launched a prototype that saved the team 20% processing time. His manager later noted: *"We didn't change Aarav's skills. We changed his belief in them."*

This story reminds us that empowerment often begins not with more ability, but with more belief. Let's now explore another vital pillar of inner empowerment: intrinsic motivation.

Intrinsic Motivation

The concept of motivation is often divided into two distinct categories: extrinsic and intrinsic. While extrinsic motivation is driven by external rewards or pressures, intrinsic motivation originates from within the individual. It is the internal drive to engage in activities for the inherent satisfaction and fulfillment they provide, rather than for some separable consequence. Understanding and fostering intrinsic motivation is crucial in empowering individuals to reach their full potential.

Intrinsic motivation is closely linked to three fundamental human needs: autonomy, competence, and relatedness. Autonomy refers to the feeling of being in control of one's own actions and decisions. When individuals perceive that they have a choice and can influence their circumstances, they are more likely to be intrinsically motivated. This sense of self-determination enhances their engagement and commitment to the task at hand.

Competence involves the feeling of being capable and effective in one's activities. When individuals feel competent, they are more likely to take on challenges and persist in the face of difficulties. This self-efficacy not only boosts intrinsic motivation but also leads to higher levels of creativity and problem-solving abilities. Providing opportunities for skill development and acknowledging achievements are effective ways to nurture a sense of competence.

Relatedness is the feeling of connection and belonging with others. Humans are inherently social beings, and fostering a sense of relatedness can significantly enhance intrinsic motivation. When individuals feel valued and understood by others, they are more likely to engage in activities that benefit both themselves and the group. Creating environments that promote collaboration and mutual support can strengthen these social bonds and, in turn, boost motivation.

Another key aspect of intrinsic motivation is the alignment of tasks with **personal values** and **interests**. When individuals find personal meaning in their activities, they are more likely to be motivated from within. This alignment not only increases engagement but also leads to greater satisfaction and well-being. Encouraging individuals to explore and pursue their passions can be a powerful way to cultivate intrinsic motivation.

The role of feedback is also significant in fostering intrinsic motivation. Constructive feedback that focuses on the process rather than the outcome helps individuals understand their progress and areas for improvement. This type of feedback supports their sense of competence and encourages a growth mindset. On the other hand, feedback that emphasizes external rewards or comparisons with others can undermine intrinsic motivation by shifting the focus away from personal growth.

Intrinsic motivation is a vital element in empowering individuals to take ownership of their learning and development. By creating environments that support autonomy, competence, and relatedness, and by aligning tasks with personal values, individuals are more likely to engage deeply with their activities. This internal drive not only enhances performance but also fosters a lifelong love of learning and personal growth. Understanding and nurturing intrinsic motivation can lead to more fulfilling and empowered lives, where individuals are driven by their own passions and aspirations rather than external pressures or rewards.

The Role of Autonomy

Autonomy is critical in personal empowerment and development in that it creates a feeling of control and ownership in one's life. Autonomy is the ability to make decisions and choices by oneself, free from external control or influence. Autonomy is encompassed in the empowering individual's concept because it allows people to take control of their lives, make informed decisions, and be accountable for their actions.

The value of autonomy is in the amount by which it can increase intrinsic motivation. When a person is autonomous, he or she will be more inclined to conduct behavior that is aligned with valued and preferred outcomes. The alignment creates a stronger commitment and interest, since the behavior is self-regulated by personal preference and not necessarily by constraint. It creates a more natural and stable type of motivation, which is needed for long-term development and growth..

Besides, autonomy also develops self-efficacy, which is the belief in being capable of performing in a given situation or accomplishing something. With autonomy in making choices, people are likely to experiment, take risks, and learn from errors. Trial and error is fundamental in building confidence and competence since it gives instant feedback of cause-and-effect to the results. This, in the long term, means a higher sense of self-efficacy, which is a key driver of success in people and their professional life.

Autonomy is also very important in generating creativity and innovation. When individuals are allowed autonomy to work on what they envision and pursue their passion without undue restrictions, they will expand their minds and generate creative solutions. Autonomy to be creative not only leads to individual satisfaction but also the greater good by building a culture of innovation and development. People are encouraged within the spaces where autonomy is valued to contribute their own ideas and assist in solving problems as a community.

Furthermore, autonomy is closely linked to emotional well-being. The ability to make choices that reflect one's true desires and needs contributes to a sense of fulfillment and satisfaction. It reduces feelings of helplessness and frustration that often accompany situations where individuals feel controlled or restricted. Autonomy supports mental health by promoting a sense of agency and empowerment, enabling individuals to take proactive steps toward achieving their goals and aspirations.

In educational and workplace settings, promoting autonomy can lead to enhanced performance and satisfaction. When students and employees are given the autonomy to choose how they approach tasks and projects, they are more likely to take ownership of their work and produce high-quality outcomes. This sense of ownership is crucial for fostering engagement and commitment, as individuals feel more invested in their work when they have a say in how it is conducted.

Lastly, the significance of autonomy in empowerment cannot be overstated. It is a foundation that constructs the stage for personal freedom, motivation, and advancement. Granting it the utmost significance will enable individuals to achieve their full potential, leading to a more purposeful and empowered existence. It is not only good for the person but also to the formation of a more vibrant and creative society. Autonomy must therefore be embraced as one of the pillars in any effort to empower and change individuals and societies.

Empowerment and Well-being

Empowerment is a multifaceted idea that goes beyond command or authority. Empowerment is creating a state of feeling valued, capable, and motivated to perform at one's best. This sense of empowerment is tied significantly to one's well-being because it creates a sense of **purpose, belongingness, and self-efficacy**. As a concept in working and personal life, empowerment is a driver of well-being in general, leading to interesting and productive lives.

The foundation of **empowerment lies in trust and respect**. When individuals are trusted to make decisions and are respected for their input, they feel a sense of ownership and responsibility. This ownership is crucial for personal growth and development, as it encourages individuals to take initiative and embrace challenges. By fostering an atmosphere of trust, organizations and communities can nurture a culture where creativity and innovation thrive, contributing to a collective sense of achievement and satisfaction.

Empowerment also involves providing the necessary resources and support for individuals to succeed. Access to information, education, and tools is essential for individuals to develop their skills and capabilities. When people are equipped with the right resources, they are more likely to feel confident and competent in their roles. This empowerment through resource allocation enhances their ability to navigate challenges and seize opportunities, leading to improved well-being and job satisfaction.

In addition, empowerment promotes active participation and engagement. Empowered people are likely to contribute to decision-making, speak up, and contribute to the discussion. Active participation instills a sense of community and cooperation, which is essential to emotional and mental health. It also minimizes isolation and despair because people know that their contribution matters.

The psychological benefits of empowerment are profound. Empowered individuals often exhibit higher levels of self-esteem and self-worth. They are more resilient in the face of adversity and are better equipped to handle stress and challenges. This resilience is a critical component of well-being, as it allows individuals to maintain a positive outlook even in difficult circumstances.

Empowerment also enhances motivation, as individuals are driven by intrinsic rewards rather than external pressures. This intrinsic motivation leads to greater satisfaction and fulfillment in both personal and professional endeavors.

Moreover, empowerment creates a chain reaction, and this effects not only the individuals but also the individuals in their immediate environment. Empowered individuals become role models, and they inspire others who desire to be empowered and live a happy life. It creates a cycle of empowerment and happiness, and it makes communities and organizations successful overall.

Empowerment is, in effect, a potent vehicle to well-being. Through the creation of a culture of trust, the offer of resources, participation, and psychological development, empowerment has the potential to build more satisfied and resilient individuals. As empowerment becomes embedded in the culture of our working and personal lives, it unlocks the floodgates to a more affluent and harmonious society with well-being within reach for everyone.

"Leading by example isn't a tactic, it's the most powerful form of influence."

— Dr. Balvinder S. Banga

Chapter - 3

Empowering Leadership for the Modern World

Leading by Example

Leadership is an art that is sustained by the fine balance between guidance and freedom. Good leadership, at its simplest level, is a matter of establishing a standard that others can look up to and emulate. It is here that the policy of leading by example comes into play, a policy that is all about demonstrating by example and not by speech.

By modeling the values and behaviors they want to see in their teams, leaders establish a culture of respect and trust. This is a leadership action style that creates a feeling of authenticity and integrity, as team members will likely mimic behaviors they see their leaders modeling. For example, a leader who shows up every day on time and ready to work creates a culture of readiness and punctuality in the team. What you do is louder and a strong behavior-influence tool that does not require coercion or micromanaging.

Leading by example is most effective in establishing a culture of accountability. If the leaders themselves maintain high standards and take responsibility for their actions, then it becomes a standard for the whole team. Not only does it encourage the team members to challenge themselves to take responsibility for their work, but it also fosters a feeling of empowerment. Empowered employees are more confident of their abilities, and due to this, there can be more job creativity, innovation, and productivity.

Additionally, leading by example is one of the methods of showing resilience and flexibility in adversity. During periods of uncertainty or crisis, a leader's frame of mind can either make or destroy the team's morale. By being calm and showing a problem-solving mindset, leaders can give their teams composure and motivation. This kind of resilience is infectious and can turn an otherwise demoralizing experience into a chance to learn and develop.

Not only for professional behavior is leading by example utilized, but also for communication and interpersonal relationships. Leaders who listen and communicate to their subordinates establish a culture of respect and inclusiveness. By valuing different perspectives and open communication, they establish a participative culture where ideas can take root. This practice not only enhances team relationships but also maximizes the performance of the whole organization.

In addition, example leading involves commitment to continuous learning and self-enhancement. Leaders committed to their own growth and their team's growth create an environment for continuous learning. This commitment to growth renders the leader and his or her team agile and poised to respond to the evolving demands of his or her industry.

In essence, leading by example is all about setting a good example and an environment where the team is valued and motivated to do their best. It is an extremely powerful strategy that motivates people by showing the path to success by example rather than command. Based on the values of integrity, accountability, and ongoing improvement, leaders are able to motivate their teams to work towards shared objectives while creating a culture of empowerment that develops through shared respect and vision.

Building Trust

Trust is the key to all relationships, both personal and business. It is the intangible tie that binds individuals together, forming cooperation, respect, and understanding. Trust is not a leadership trait anyone would desire but a necessity that can make or destroy a whole organization.

Leaders who focus on building trust provide a platform for open communication and openness. Openness gives team members comfort to share ideas, voice concerns, and make contributions to group objectives without fear of being criticized or retaliated against. Trust thus becomes an enabler of innovation, allowing free exchange of ideas and creativity.

Establishing trust starts with showing consistency of action and word. Leaders have to get their words and actions on the same page and follow through on their commitments no matter how insignificant the commitment. That dependability provides team members with a sense of security and a feeling that they can trust the genuineness of intent of their leader. When people feel secure, they are more likely to become all they can become and put their energies into what is being done.

Another most critical role in establishing trust is the capacity to listen sincerely. Leaders need to learn to listen so that they can hear the views and requirements of their people. Listening actively is not merely hearing the words, it is sympathetic comprehension of the emotions and motivations that lie behind the words. By appreciating alternative viewpoints and demonstrating empathy, leaders make it clear that they respect and esteem every member's input.

Also, empowerment strengthens trust. Empowering the members of the team by the leaders conveys a message of confidence and belief in them. Empowerment means delegating power, providing the necessary resources, and making one feel the ownership of their job. This boosts the morale as well as creates a culture of trust in which the members of the team feel valued and trusted enough to make decisions.

Transparency is also among the pillars of building trust. The leaders must try to keep things open and honest with the teams. Organizational purpose or challenges/shifts aside, transparency keeps the team members informed and aligned with the vision of the leader. Transparency reduces uncertainty and creates a shared understanding that helps in building strengthened trust.

Accountability is also required in establishing trust. Leaders must hold themselves and their followers accountable for results and behaviors. By establishing clear expectations and providing constructive feedback, leaders provide for responsibility and integrity. Once individuals understand accountability is a mutual principle, they will be more apt to trust the fairness and objectivity of their leader.

Building trust is not one action, but rather a continuous process that requires determination and intentionality. By building trust with their teams, leaders are laying the groundwork for a strong and cohesive organizational culture. Such a culture is resistant to adversity but is made even stronger through cooperation and respect. Lastly, by building trust, leaders allow their teams to thrive, the whole being more than any parts.

Encouraging Initiative

In a world where obedience and conformity are so highly valued, developing a culture that values initiative can be a revolutionary thing. Initiative is not action, it's being open to going beyond normal confines and establishing new horizons. It is the foundation of personal development and organizational success, and it produces innovation and increased problem-solving capacity.

Creating an environment that nurtures initiative begins with cultivating a mindset that values curiosity and creativity. Encouraging individuals to question the status quo and propose new ideas not only enriches the workplace or community but also empowers people to take ownership of their roles. When individuals feel that their contributions are valued and that their ideas can lead to real change, they are more likely to take the initiative.

Leaders themselves have a major role to play in generating such a culture. They must lead by example, being open to new ideas and willing to take calculated risks. By designing failure not as an objective but as a learning experience, leaders can remove the fear of failure that stifles initiative at its inception. Appreciation and encouragement must be substituted by criticism and punishment, and experimentation and learning must be allowed in a risk-free environment.

Practical strategies for encouraging initiative include setting clear goals while allowing flexibility in how those goals are achieved. Rather than dictating every step, leaders can provide the "what" and the "why," leaving the "how" to the ingenuity of their team. This approach not only fosters creativity but also allows individuals to develop problem-solving skills and confidence in their abilities.

Moreover, recognizing and rewarding initiative is essential. Celebrating successes, no matter how small, reinforces the value of taking proactive steps and encourages others to follow suit. Recognition can take many forms, from public acknowledgment to opportunities for professional development or increased responsibility.

Training and development opportunities are also vital in encouraging initiative. Providing resources and learning experiences equips individuals with the skills and knowledge needed to take action. Workshops, mentorship programs, and cross-functional projects can broaden perspectives and inspire new ways of thinking.

Communication is another cornerstone of encouraging initiative. Open channels of communication ensure that ideas can be shared freely and that feedback is both given and received constructively. Regular meetings and brainstorming sessions can serve as platforms for sharing ideas and fostering collaboration, creating a dynamic interchange of thoughts that can lead to innovative solutions.

Lastly, purpose can highly inspire initiative. If people know how their job helps achieve the organization's or society's greater goals, they will be more likely to take action. Work with purpose is fulfilling and inspiring to do more than is required..

In its simplest form, inspiring initiative is about empowering the other person to think for himself or herself. Leadership is an art that is learned through the fine balance of guidance and autonomy. In fact, effective leadership is all about setting an example that the other person can look up to and emulate. This is where the concept of leading by example comes in, a concept that focuses so much more on action than on word.

When leaders demonstrate what they want their teams to embody, they create a culture of trust and respect. This is a culture of integrity and authenticity because team members are going to emulate behaviors they observe in their leaders. For instance, a leader who arrives on time and is prepared sends a message of discipline and effectiveness to the team. Actions are louder than words and are a powerful behavior driver without having to use coercion and micromanaging.

Empowering leadership often starts with trust and a simple question: '**What do you think**?' The transformation at Revathi's warehouse shows how small shifts lead to massive impact.

📓 Case Story: "Revathi's Turnaround Team"

In a Pune-based mid-sized logistics firm, the warehouse optimization department was notorious for tardiness and aloofness. When Revathi took over the department, she implemented three changes on the spot:

- Showed punctuality and conciseness in all meetings (leading by example)
- Held open Q&A huddles weekly (trust-building)
- Asked the floor staff for new floor planning concepts (encouraging initiative)

Her approach encouraged technician Amit to propose a low-cost path optimization model. It saved ₹12 lakhs in 6 months. When she publicly disclosed his success and provided him with software training, others also got inspired. The warehouse output improved by 38% in a year.

Amit afterwards stated, "*No one had ever asked us for suggestions before. Revathi made us feel like we could also lead.*"

<u>These stories show that when individuals are observed and praised, initiative is spontaneous. Let us now see how</u>

leaders can maintain this energy through feedback and continuous praise.

Feedback and Support

Feedback and guidance in the context of empowerment is of utmost significance. Not only does it help in individual as well as professional development, but it also generates respect and trust culture. Constructive criticism is a very effective means of individual development. It informs individuals about their strengths and weaknesses and offers them chances for constant improvement.

The most important part of effective feedback is its timing, specificity, and tone. Timing gives feedback relevance and usefulness, and individuals can do something about suggestions right away in their jobs. Specificity is highlighting certain actions or outcomes and not stating generalities. It makes it simple for the recipients to fully understand precisely what to alter or enhance.

There must be an empathetic tone when providing feedback. Effort awareness and empathy towards the receiver as well can have a tremendous impact on the acceptability of feedback.

Constructive criticism must be balanced with encouragement, acknowledging both failure and success. It not only encourages but also reminds people of their worth and potential.

Support, as a complement to feedback, is an empowerment key too. It is about providing people with the resources, instruction, and encouragement they require to implement feedback. Support can take many forms, ranging from extra training and resources to a culture where people feel comfortable to experiment and take risks.

An open line of communication is a very key aspect of support. Open discussion facilitated makes one feel that they are understood and heard, and that they belong. Openness enables people to be able to discuss ideas and ask questions without feeling judged.

Mentorship is another invaluable source of assistance, offering anyone the chance to learn from the experience and insights of others. A mentor can offer individual advice, impart information, and navigate one through challenging situations, serving as a source of direction for one on the journey to empowerment.

The feedback and support roles of leaders also cannot be overemphasized. Leaders set the tone for organizational culture, and their feedback is priceless in establishing a culture of promoting development and growth. Leaders, in demonstrating good feedback and support behaviors, can inspire others to do so, and in doing so, establish a continuous improvement culture.

Also, leaders have to develop a feedback-rich culture that allows all, regardless of position, to give and receive feedback openly. This democratic feedback style ensures inclusiveness since all voices are heard, and diverse input is appreciated, making the collaborative process richer.

Becoming part of the culture of an organization or society requires a commitment to continuous learning and adaptation. It involves recognizing that empowerment is not an isolated act but a process that evolves in tandem with the aspirations and needs of the people.

Lastly, feedback and support are not simply tools of support but are inherent in the empowerment process. They offer the scaffolding upon which people can construct their capabilities, enabling a culture in which everyone is empowered to give their best. This feedback/support synergy translates potential into performance, reinforcing the empowerment ethos without dominating it.

"True collaboration emerges when every voice matters and shared goals guide every action."

— Dr. Balvinder S. Banga

Chapter - 4

Collaborative Empowerment: Building High- Trust Teams

Collaborative Environment

Empowerment is a multifaceted concept that is at the heart of leadership and individual growth. It is essentially about giving individuals or groups the resources, tools, and authority to take charge of their lives and make choices that will determine their destiny. This is a concept that transcends the mere delegation of work; it is a deeper articulation of trust, respect, and cooperation that sets the tone where people feel respected and empowered.

The empowerment ethos is the merging of support and autonomy. Empowerment calls for a move away from conventional hierarchical structures to an inclusive and participative one. In an empowered setting, people are inspired to make their opinions heard, to offer ideas, and to be accountable. Not only does this participative process contribute to people's individual development, but it also strengthens the group's or organization's collective power.

The most critical element of empowerment is establishing self-efficacy, that is, people feeling that they are capable of doing something. When people are empowered, they will challenge themselves, stay motivated in the face of challenges, and achieve their goals. This sense of self-efficacy tends to be established as a result of being offered the proper training, proper equipment, and chances for personal as well as professional development.

Empowerment also comes with the concept of accountability. When individuals are empowered, they will be held accountable for the decisions and actions they take. Such accountability begets responsibility and commitment, and this could lead to improved performance and productivity. Moreover, when individuals are held accountable, they are likely to learn and keep on improving, thereby increasing their competencies and skills.

Empowerment, in the context of leadership, is the act of creating an environment in which the feeling of being valued and respected by team members is enabled. Empowering leaders are able to spot positive strengths in people and use them to propel collective goals. Empowering leaders lead and advise but give team members the freedom of learning and innovating. Empowering leadership not only boosts morale but also triggers creativity and innovation, and the organization becomes stronger and more dynamic.

The benefits of empowerment do not end at organizational and individual development. Empowerment also has significant implications for social and economic development. Empowered individuals are more likely to participate actively in their communities, advocate for change, and contribute to the overall well-being of society. This ripple effect can result in more equitable and sustainable development outcomes, particularly in marginalized or disadvantaged groups.

However, empowerment is not without its challenges. It requires a cultural shift and a reversal of existing power dynamics. ***Resistance to change, fear of loss of control, and lack of trust can hinder the empowerment process***. Therefore, it is essential to foster an environment of openness and transparency, where communication is encouraged and feedback is valued. By addressing these challenges, organizations and communities can create a more inclusive and empowering environment for all.

In summary, empowerment is a dynamic and transformative process that enables individuals and groups to realize their full potential. It is a powerful tool for fostering personal growth, enhancing organizational effectiveness, and driving social change. By understanding and embracing the principles of empowerment, we can create a more equitable and sustainable future for everyone. A successful collaborative culture is not merely a company where everyone gets along; it is a culture that is built upon mutual respect, open communication, and shared goals. In the work environment, establishing this kind of culture is a system-wide effort and a reflective style of leadership in which empowering others is more vital than controlling them.

One of the vital features of a team setting is the appreciation of various viewpoints and strengths. Every member of the team brings along his or her strengths and ideas, which, when utilized in a proper way, can be utilized to achieve innovative solutions as well as higher productivity. Diversity is not just about embracing differences but even transcending that to comprehend and incorporate them into the common goal. This can contribute to a strengthened and flexible team that is capable of resolving complex problems with a holistic approach.

Open communication is another foundation of a **collaborative culture.** It entails establishing avenues through which communication is left open and ideas are shared without fear of retaliation. Leaders lead by being open to input and accessible themselves. They have to make members feel comfortable expressing their views and ideas, creating a culture where criticism is seen as a chance to learn and not as a threat. Openness creates trust and facilitates the development of the idea that all feedback is appreciated, encouraging people to interact more actively with one another.

Shared objectives play a crucial role in bringing together the efforts of a team. When all of them understand and are bound by a common goal, their joint efforts become more focused and substantial. Leaders need to do so by communicating the vision clearly and ensuring everyone understands how they fit into the mechanism of achieving it. Regular review of these objectives and monitoring progress can keep things in motion and ensure everyone remains on the right path.

Apart from that, mutual respect enables a culture of teamwork. **Valuing each other's time, intellect, and effort enables a feeling of belongingness and oneness**. It transcends professionalism to value the personal life and well-being of the employees. Flexible working hours, valuing one's effort, and encouraging work-life balance are practices that demonstrate respect and empathy, which further enables collaborative culture.

Technology also plays an important part in enabling collaboration. Communication, project management, and information-sharing technologies cannot be substituted in today's workplace.

However, technology has to support, not replace, the human elements of teamwork. As much as possible, digital platforms can increase reach and simplify processes, yet they have to be used to enhance, not overshadow, the interpersonal relationships that are the foundation of a collaborative environment.

Finally, creating a culture of collaboration is an ongoing process. It must be cultivated and perfected continually in accordance with evolving situations and team dynamics. The leaders must be ever vigilant, continuously assessing the health of the collaborative culture, and be proactive in solving any problems that might arise. By empowering, not controlling, they can create a strong and innovative team capable of producing outstanding results.

By doing this, a collaborative culture is an effective means of **organizational and individual development**, achieving success that is inclusive and sustainable. The power of such a culture is that it can tap into the collective power of its members and transform it into a force for good and change.

Shared Vision

In any partnership, the common vision is the cornerstone upon which good working partnerships are grounded. It is the common perception and alignment of values, goals, and aspirations that drive a group to a common goal. The strength of a common vision is that it is capable of consolidating the different perceptions and abilities of every member, converging to a common agenda.

Shared vision is less about setting a list of goals that everyone agrees to and more about establishing a culture in which everyone has something to say and ideas are on the table. It is a dynamic process, evolving as the team grows and matures, and it requires continuous conversation and reflection. With open communication, individuals can express their ideas and concerns, making a more whole and inclusive vision. Open practice of this kind makes everyone feel heard and invested in the product, encouraging motivation and buy-in.

The formation of a common vision begins with the distinct articulation of the larger purpose. Leaders spearhead the process of setting the stage for collaboration, promoting openness, and establishing trust. They must form platforms where different points of view are communicated, resulting in creativity and innovation. Through this, they are not only inspiring but also empowering members of their teams to contribute their own strengths and ideas.

A proper shared vision is one that is clear and relevant. It is a guide that steers decision-making and prioritization so that activities are targeted and aligned with the master objectives. Furthermore, it is a source of inspiration, inducing a sense of belonging and purpose among the team members. When individuals understand how their contribution fits into the big picture, they will be more likely to own responsibility for their roles and obligations.

Also, shared vision is dynamic. It has to be revisited and updated constantly to be responsive to the changing world. Teams should be adaptable enough to adjust and change their vision when new challenges and opportunities present themselves. Flexibility is critical in sustaining momentum and in developing sustainability.

In reality, building a shared vision is a process of building step by step. It starts with discovering the underlying values and principles that will inspire the team. These are the building blocks that are employed to formulate realistic and attainable goals. Second, open lines of communication are employed to facilitate collaboration and feedback. Frequent meetings and feedback sessions allow for reviewing and readjusting, keeping the vision alive and current.

It is only when there is commitment by each of the members and a sense of compromise and shared-ness that there can be a shared vision. Through seeing and respecting the diversity of experience and opinion of the team members, a stronger and more sustainable vision can be built. This shared process not only makes the outcomes more quality-oriented but also connects the team members more strongly.

Finally, shared vision is a great way of empowering individuals and teams. It brings a culture of respect, collaboration, and support in which every individual can perform their best. With shared goals and principles, teams can overcome challenges with confidence and accomplish successes together. This is what characterizes an empowered team where every individual feels empowered and motivated to contribute positively.

In today's adaptive workplaces, teamwork isn't merely working together it's seeing together. Authentic empowerment is not derived from formal structures, but from a mindset to listen, relate, and evolve. Often the most potent transformation does not initiate in the boardroom it starts on the shop floor. *A perfect example is the story of a Pune-based architecture company.*

📘 The Harmony Blueprint: A Story of Grassroots Collaboration

There was no paucity of talent at a mid-sized Pune architecture firm—so were the problems. The design, operations, and finance departments communicated in silos. With each one having their own specialized know-how, deadlines were missed and morale fell. The firm was losing its momentum not because of lack of skill, but lack of alignment.

And Project Harmony, not started from the C-suite but by Priya, an in-the-middle design lead with a modest proposal, a one-hour weekly meeting called "Shared Wins & Woes." Teams gathered every Friday, without slides, status updates, and pomp, to speak openly—what went well, what didn't, and what could be changed.

What unfolded was transformative?

- The **finance team** confirmed they used to receive delayed operations data, impacting budget preparation.
- **Operations** realized that they did not know the entire design process or timeline.
- The **design** team understood that late drawings weren't creative delays—vendor payments and client trust were affected by them.

And as open discussion supplanted assumptions, trust grew. Silos disintegrated. What started as an ad hoc habit caught the eye of leadership? They made it official— the facilitator rotation, a visual "***Shared Vision Charter***" in every department, and Friday sessions that became a benchmark of their culture.

Within three months, the company initiated two significant projects in advance of time. The most important thing wasn't new technology and methodology it ***was conversation, trust and solidarity.***

Project Harmony showed that genuine collaboration is not hierarchical it just needs a human touch.

Project Harmony is proof that collective empowerment is not a **top-down directive, but a culture created through the development of trust, conversation, and shared intention**. When people feel that they are safe to speak and are being listened to intentionally, even the most complex organizations can access flow, creativity, and momentum. It reminds us that change begins with conversation and enduring change is a team sport.

Open Communication

Effective communication is the basis for empowering relationships, both in personal life and in work life. Open communication is the exchange of information freely, truthfully, and respectfully. Open communication is an essential factor in building trust, understanding, and collaboration.

In an empowered relationship, there is open communication, and all parties involved can freely express their thoughts, feelings, and concerns without fear of judgment or even punishment. In this kind of communication, active listening is encouraged, and everyone is concerned to hear what the other has to say. Active listening is not just hearing words; you are listening for non-verbal cues such as body language and voice tone, which tell you even more than what you hear from the mouth.

Open communication also **involves accuracy and clarity** of communication. Openness may result in misunderstandings, which may result in mistrust or conflict, when there is vagueness and ambiguity. Being **clear and accurate ensures that one's message is delivered** as intended, reducing possibilities of being misunderstood. Clarity helps in creating realistic expectations and ensures effective problem-solving.

Second, open communication has the attribute of feedback, which is **crucial for growth and development**. *Positive feedback, if offered tactfully, can help individuals and teams identify areas of improvement and strengths. Feedback must be offered positively, talking about the* *behavior and not the individual, thus fostering a culture of support where individuals feel appreciated and respected.*

furthermore, open communication encourages diversity and inclusivity of ideas. By offering an arena where different ideas are accepted and embraced, individuals tend to develop creative ideas and solutions. Diversity enhances decision-making processes and leads to more effective and inclusive solutions. In the workplace, encouraging an inclusive culture of communication can foster creativity and innovation, thus organizational success.

Power dynamics, cultural differences, and personal prejudices may create barriers to communication. These have to be recognized and bridged to create a free communication culture. Culturally aware communication involves awareness of communication style and cultural differences. As long as there is awareness of potential power imbalance, people can strive to create a more even communication space where all are heard.

With the advent of the age of technology, communication has been dominated by technology. Although digital media are convenient and easy to adapt to, they are also problematic for open communication. Tone and intention tend to be more easily misconstrued through textual communication, and caution in language use and context is therefore required. Video conferencing software can overcome this through observation of body language, but intentionality in interaction is needed to make open communication possible.

Lastly, ***open communication is something that requires to be maintained with consistent effort and commitment***. It is a process of developing a culture of openness, respect, and trust in which individuals feel comfortable expressing themselves and listening to others. Placing a premium on open communication enables relationships to grow, enables conflict to be resolved in a positive manner, and enables collaborative work to lead to great achievements. **Open communication in personal and professional relationships is not merely a tool to an end but a natural supporting beam of empowerment**.

Celebrating Success

Recognizing and celebrating success naturally occurs in building positive culture, whether personal growth, academic culture, or corporate culture. Recognizing success, both small and large, is one of the strong drivers of increasing enthusiasm, rewarding good behavior, and creating a culture of appreciation and encouragement. It is important to have a knowledge of the science of celebrating success to inspire, not intimidate, individuals and groups.

Festivalizing success can be seen as a platform to remind people of the values and objectives that define a group or individual's aspirations. Success, if it occurs, is tangible evidence of the goals established and work put into accomplishing them. Not just motivational, it also provides a benchmark for comparison of future effort. By placing in front of them what they have accomplished, people and groups are able to determine how far they have reached and where they may improve or innovate further.

Having celebrations as a part of the calendar assists in the creation of a culture in which achievements are enjoyed and not assumed. It promotes a culture of celebrating wins no matter how minute and remaining optimistic. When individuals feel that their work makes a difference, they are more likely to be committed and involved. This is especially crucial in environments where extended projects or schemes need to be worked on with steady effort and dedication.

It is important to personalize celebrations according to the nature of the achievement and the preferences of the people being celebrated. Personalizing recognition ensures that it will be significant to the people themselves, and therefore, even more effective. This may be as casual as an oral acknowledgment in a meeting, or as formalized as award ceremonies or team celebrations. What is most significant is to make sure that the mode of celebration is in line with the values and culture of the team, so that it feels natural and not elitist.

Theory is one thing transformation is quite another that requires working through resistance, obstacles, and the nuances of human nature. To demonstrate the strength of grit, shared accountability, and trust-based leadership, I'd like to offer a personal story of how collaborative empowerment can reclaim not only a project, but a culture..

☆ The Story of Project Vijayant: From Breakdown to Breakthrough

Case Study | By Dr. Balvinder S. Banga, CTO

When one of India's top Mumbai-based logistics firms rolled out Project Vijayant, **the vision was ambitious**: to digitally optimize internal operations through a workflow platform that brought everything together. As CTO, I felt that this digitalization had the ability to revolutionize the way we worked streamlined, integrated, future-proof.

But it wasn't easy to succeed.

The Biggest Challenge? Insufficient Cooperation.

Even after a few cycles of pre-launch training, the **department heads were resistant to change. Silos continued**. Alignment did not happen. In fact, the initial few weeks saw a business disruption of significant scale, with workflows getting disrupted and team morale low. Three or four months of sustained effort were needed to realign vision, re-build bridges, and build momentum.

My IT team, motivated solely by passion, worked around the clock sometimes literally hand in hand with each and every other department. We listened, re-planned, streamlined, and re-trained. We transformed not only the tool but the culture.

A breakthrough came with the introduction of daily recognition ceremonies. A junior analyst was rewarded for identifying a major data gap. An engineer was thanked for backend load times optimization. These recognitions sparked energy and trust.

Festivals became a norm. Respect across functions increased. Gradually, Vijayant turned from a system into a symbol of what can be achieved when individuals come together, have a stake, and believe in change.

This change wasn't brought about by code or design it was brought about by empowered collaboration.

Hands Behind Vijayant Project

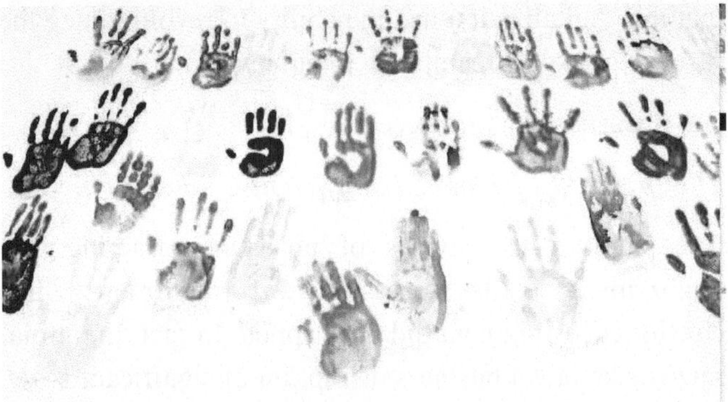

Project Vijayant's turnaround was not just a technological success—it was a testament to what's possible when empowered leadership meets collaborative intent. It reminds us that empowerment doesn't begin with process; it begins with people. True collaboration requires courage, trust, and the humility to re-align, even after failure. As leaders, it is our responsibility to foster environments where trust can grow, and from that trust, transformation emerges.

Moreover, celebrating success should not be limited to final outcomes. Recognizing the process and the effort put into the journey is equally important. By acknowledging milestones along the way, individuals and teams can maintain momentum and stay focused on their objectives. This approach fosters a culture where learning and growth are prioritized, and where setbacks are viewed as opportunities for development rather than failures.

Another critical aspect of celebrating success is inclusivity. It is essential to ensure that all contributions are recognized, regardless of their scale. This promotes a sense of belonging and equality within the group, as everyone feels valued for their input. Celebrations should highlight the diversity of skills and perspectives that contribute to success, fostering a collaborative environment where everyone's efforts are seen and appreciated.

Ultimately, the celebration of success should empower individuals and teams to continue striving for excellence. By creating a culture that values recognition, organizations and communities can inspire confidence and foster a sense of purpose among their members. This empowerment leads to greater innovation, productivity, and satisfaction, as individuals feel motivated to push boundaries and achieve their full potential.

In conclusion, celebrating success is not merely a formality or a reward, but a strategic tool for empowerment. It is a critical component of any approach that seeks to inspire and motivate individuals and teams, ensuring that they feel valued and supported in their endeavors. By embracing a culture of celebration, we can unlock the potential within ourselves and those around us, paving the way for continued growth and achievement.

"Education should empower minds, not just fill them."

— Dr. Balvinder S. Banga

Chapter - 5

Educator as Enabler- Empowering Learning Environments

Student-Centered Learning

In a time when education is evolving so rapidly, the focus is shifting increasingly toward approaches that are student-centered. Student-centered learning, a pedagogy that positions the student at the center of the learning process, is becoming increasingly popular as educators seek to engage learning in a more interactive and productive manner. This form of learning reconfigures the traditional teacher-student model by establishing space in which students are active agents in their own learning.

Fundamentally, student-centered learning is about individual growth and comprehension rather than repetition of the same thing again and again. It motivates learners to learn topics in their own way of interest, engaging with topics at a higher level. It acknowledges that every learner is different, with differences in learning styles, learning pace, and learning preferences. By having such respect for differences, instructors can more easily customize approaches to fit individual needs, improving learning.

One of the foundations of student-centered learning is the acquisition of critical thinking. Rather than passive reception of information, students are directed to evaluate, analyze, and synthesize information. This allows for more profound comprehension and application of the subject matter, and students are able to apply the knowledge in practical situations. Through the acquisition of these skills, teachers prepare students to think for themselves and be lifelong learners.

The second key component of this strategy is teamwork and communication. Learning in the student-led classroom often happens through teamwork, discussion, and peer-to-peer exchange. The process of teamwork learning not only contributes to better understanding but also to productive social skills. Students are able to share themselves, listen, and collaborate for common purposes, preparing them for future teamwork in their careers and personal lives.

Student-centered learning is also different from the conventional when it comes to evaluation. Instead of using standardized tests, teachers utilize a set of tools to assess a student's learning process. These tools comprise a portfolio, project assessment, and reflective journals. These tools provide a wider picture of a student's capability and progress, which allows for accurate evaluation of their strengths and weaknesses.

Technology becomes a central element in facilitating student-centered learning. Technology and web-based resources give students the platform to study subjects beyond the classroom. Web-based websites offer individualized learning plans, with access to a vast reservoir of data and interactive materials. Such inclusion of technology not only maximizes learning, but also prepares students for a technology-driven world.

But student-centered learning has its own set of challenges as well. It requires a shift in attitude on the part of students and teachers. The teachers must learn to relinquish some control and take on the role of the facilitator and not the authority model. For the students, it requires more personal responsibility and self-motivation. But if it is done properly, the reward is well worth the struggle in the form of a more vibrant and inclusive learning community.

Finally, student-centered learning redefines the learning environment by putting the learner at center stage. Through the creation of a discovery culture, working together, and analytical thinking, it enables the learner to own learning, bringing about an active, informed, and empowered generation. Not only does it raise academic achievement, but it also empowers learners with the ability to negotiate the plots of an evolving world. By empowering learners, education is no longer merely a tool of individual and society advancement.

Empowerment in education often transcends textbooks and test scores. Sometimes, it means recognizing the quiet voice in the room and handing it a microphone. My son, Mansidak, taught me this lesson not in a classroom but on a martial arts mat.

Empowerment Beyond the Classroom – Mansidak's Martial Arts Journey

Mansidak had always been a reserved boy—more observer than participant. Sports days came and went. He admired others but never stepped forward.

Until one day, he timidly asked if he could try **martial arts**. We enrolled him in a beginner's class, just to see.

What followed was nothing short of transformation.

Each day after school, he practiced diligently—**falling, getting up, trying again**. His confidence grew not with medals, but with **every belt he earned**. He learned to control his emotions, focus his mind, and respect both competition and self.

At his first tournament, he didn't win. But he stood tall, calm, and proud. Not because he was the strongest—but because he **chose to fight**, not just an opponent, but his fears.

Mansidak's journey reminds us that when children are trusted to take ownership of their learning, they don't just build skills—they build identity. In empowering environments, learners find not just answers, but themselves.

Encouraging Critical Thinking

In a world that is information-overloaded, critical thinking is more valuable than ever before. Critical thinking enables us to cut through the muddle of modern life with wisdom and insight. It is not only a mental skill but also a life skill that helps us make informed decisions, solve problems in a best possible manner, and understand the consequences of our actions.

The building of critical thinking starts with creating a platform for inquiry and questioning. It starts with building an open-minded thinking attitude towards problem-solving and learning. Promoting people to question, look for different views, and question assumptions sets the foundation for critical thinking. Not only does this improve cognitive capacity, but confidence in analyzing and interpreting also develops.

One strong method of encouraging critical thinking is providing the opportunity for debate and discussion. Discussion with others introduces people to varying viewpoints and compels them to think about opposing views. This type of mental interaction hones analytical ability and helps to identify bias and flaws in argument. Facilitators of such debating should encourage respectful opposition and encourage participants to back up assertions with evidence.

Promoting skepticism and healthy skepticism is also an essential element. It is essential to educate people in order to assess the authenticity and reliability of sources, particularly in a period when disinformation is so prevalent. Giving people the tools to check the validity of information equips them with the ability to distinguish fact from opinion, thus allowing them to make decisions based on facts.

Problem-solving exercises are also an excellent means of creating critical thinking. Presenting scenarios that require creative solutions compels individuals to apply their learning in the real world. The exercises should be capable of challenging the participants to think creatively and come up with multiple solutions before a conclusion is reached. This not only enhances critical thinking but also resilience and flexibility.

In addition, incorporating reflective practices into daily life can tremendously enhance critical thinking. Requesting people to reflect on their thought patterns, decisions, and results allows them to realize their intellectual flaws and areas for improvement. Self-reflection promotes a culture of ongoing learning and self-enhancement, which is critical in building effective critical thinking skills.

Schools and the work environment also need to play their part in enhancing critical thinking. School curricula that emphasize inquiry and problem-solving over memorization are likely to produce individuals with the ability to think critically. Work environments that encourage innovation and openness to diverse inputs also provide an environment where critical thinking is fostered.

Finally, we want to empower people to be independent thinkers and decision-makers in their own right. By promoting the spirit of inquiry and giving people tools to critically evaluate information, we equip them to meet the challenges of the modern world confidently and competently. **Critical thinking is not a skill alone** but an attitude which, once cultivated, releases a whole potential and helps people contribute meaningfully to society. Empowerment and not over-powering with predetermined solutions leads to **growth, innovation, and development**..

Teacher as Facilitator

With the changing education scenario, the role of the teacher has also undergone tremendous change. Traditionally the fount of knowledge, the teacher was very much an authoritative personality, imparting knowledge and judging students on how well they were able to absorb and repeat knowledge. But with contemporary educational philosophies, there is a strong trend towards a student-centric model where the teacher plays more of a facilitator's role than a director of learning.

Instructional facilitation rests on the assumption that learning is an active, dynamic process. It assumes students will learn best when they are active, questioning, and capable of investigating matters in the manner most productive for their own learning style. To this degree, the teacher's role is to create an environment that encourages exploration and assists the students in their quest for knowledge.

The single most significant aspect of being a facilitator is creating an inclusive classroom climate. This involves creating a classroom where the students feel safe, valued, and respected, and where their ideas and opinions are heard. By creating a positive classroom climate, the teacher can enable the students to feel comfortable to express themselves, cooperate with others, and think critically. This not only enhances the learning outcomes but enables the students to develop their confidence and interpersonal skills.

Besides, teacher-facilitators guide students to become problem solvers and independent thinkers. Instead of presenting students with pre-packaged answers, facilitators pose open questions that push students to think for themselves and consider things from many different angles. By this, students are accountable and self-driven through making what they have learned their own responsibility.

As facilitators to learning, teachers are also guides, helping students navigate through information and resources. In the era of the internet, where there is so much information, students typically need help on how to identify sources of information that are credible and how to successfully integrate information. Teachers function as facilitators to guide them through in presenting tools and approaches to successful research and critical thinking.

The shift to facilitation requires teachers' adaptability and flexibility. This requires sensitivity to the diversity of needs among the students and adaptableness in adjusting teaching approaches to enhance the fit with diverse learning styles. It also demands openness to new technologies and approaches that will enhance the learning process. Through adaptability, facilitators will make their teaching beneficial and effective in a dynamic learning environment.

In addition, the facilitator model is interested in the worth of collaboration. Teachers collaborate with students, learning from and with them, rather than lecturing in a commanding role. There is a respect for one another and a consensus in working for learning in this collaborative dynamic.

In the end, the facilitator teacher exists to empower students. By assisting them in identifying their areas of strength and interest, students are left with a passion for learning that can extend beyond their school days to last a lifetime. Empowerment in this sense is not about relinquishing control but about distributing control so that students will be active learners in their own education. By doing so, teachers are not only preparing students for academic success in the classroom but also for the challenges and opportunities of the wider world.

Empowering Curriculum

An Empowering curriculum is the foundation for the development of independent learners and active participants in the learning process. It is an innovative teaching approach that shifts the emphasis from memorization to establishing **critical thinking, creativity, and problem-solving skills**. The strategy fosters confidence and ownership by making the learner the owner of the learning process.

At the core of an empowering curriculum is the assumption that students are not passive recipients of knowledge. They are rather engaged participants in their own learning process, capable of influencing and enriching their own learning experience. It values students' diverse talents and interests to such an extent that students can become more engaged and substantive in their learning.

A self-empowering curriculum goes beyond instruction. Project-based learning is used where students are confronted with real-life challenges and collaborate to develop solutions. This hands-on experience not only improves learning but also builds critical thinking skills like **teamwork, communication, and adaptability**. Projects allow students to tackle complex issues, critically analyze potential solutions, and implement their ideas.

Furthermore, an empowering curriculum offers means for students to become agents of learning. By choice and flexibility in the way they engage in assignments, students have agency and control over learning. This can be accomplished through various avenues, including independent research projects, student passion-based electives, and the ability to pursue topics beyond the standard curriculum.

Technology integration is also a key aspect of an empowering curriculum. Technology and digital tools offer new means of searching and creating. Students are able to locate enormous amounts of information, collaborate with others in other parts of the world, and present learning in multimedia reports, computer code, and digital stories. Technology is a bridge, linking students to a larger world of information and ideas.

Assessment in an empowering curriculum is also distinct in character. Rather than employing conventional tests, assessment is made reflective and integrated. Portfolios, presentations, and peer assessment present a clearer image of a student's growth and potential. This activity is learning-centered as an ongoing process, and students are encouraged to reflect on their progress and establish personal goals.

Teachers are important in developing an empowering curriculum. Teachers are guides and facilitators who establish a secure environment where students feel at ease to experiment and try out new concepts. Teachers are motivated to develop a culture of curiosity and inquiry by engaging in open-ended questioning, discussions, and encouraging open dialogue. This energy exchange between the teacher and student creates a classroom culture where learning is social and communal.

Finally, an empowering curriculum teaches students to face the complexity of the modern world. With the right knowledge and attitude to adapt to the changing world, students are more likely to succeed in their later lives. Not only is this improving the academic performance, but it is also enhancing the creation of well-rounded citizens able to positively contribute to society. ***Education is thus being converted into an instrument of empowerment, which can unleash capability as well as enable lifelong learning***.

"Parenting is not about control—it's about creating space for children to find their own strength."

— Dr. Balvinder S. Banga

Chapter - 6

Empowerment in Parenting

Setting Boundaries

Understanding the significance of boundaries is important for healthy relationships and personal growth. Boundaries are boundaries which we establish in order to protect and honor our personal space, feelings, and values. Boundaries are required in order to have balance within relationships, so our needs are also taken care of and the needs of others. Setting boundaries is not about building walls to exclude people but establishing a safe environment in which respect and understanding can grow.

In human relationships, boundaries set the dynamics of the individuals towards one another. They are guidelines of proper behavior and communication, hence guaranteeing that each person is valued and respected. By communicating our boundaries clearly, we prevent misunderstandings and conflicts arising from unfulfilled needs. Healthy boundaries form open communication, wherein both parties are free to state their needs and concerns without fear of judgment or attack.

At work, boundaries are also necessary. They define roles and responsibilities, preventing burnout and maintaining a healthy working environment. Working within boundaries at workplace means time management, well-delegating tasks, and maintaining a work-life balance. It means knowing how to say no to more responsibilities that could cost one's health and performance. By establishing boundaries, employees are able to concentrate on their work without the additional stress of over commitment.

Self-care involves boundaries too. Boundaries are necessary so that one could prioritize one's own mental, emotional, and physical well-being by having some time to rest, reflect, and recharge. Establishing boundaries here involves acknowledging one's own limitations and speaking up for one's own needs. It involves acknowledging that self-care is not selfish but rather a part of a meaningful life. By taking care of oneself, one could serve others better and be of positive value to society.

Boundaries must be communicated clearly and consistently in order to work. This is accomplished by being assertive while remaining respectful in the communication of one's needs and also boundaries. It also involves being open to listening and adaptable with other people's boundaries. Consistency is the most crucial aspect, if boundaries are not enforced consistently, then they don't work and lead to confusion and resentment.

It is hard to set boundaries, particularly for people who are not accustomed to speaking up for themselves. You must have self-awareness and the courage to tolerate uncomfortable moments. But the benefits of healthy boundaries are well worth the discomfort. They lead to more satisfying relationships, improved mental well-being, and increased freedom and autonomy in one's life.

Lastly, boundaries empower. They enable us to take responsibility for our lives, make deliberate choices, and create spaces that nourish our well-being. By establishing and respecting boundaries, we create spaces in which everyone can thrive, founded on respect and understanding. By doing so, we empower ourselves and others, creating the condition for more harmonious and satisfying interactions.

Encouraging Independence

Fostering independence in human beings is a critical component of work-life and personal development. It is a matter of walking the thin line between guiding and allowing independence so that people find their potential, make decisions, and learn from errors. Fostering independence is about developing the setting one where trust, accountability, and independence are fostered.

The foundation of autonomy is built on trust. When people feel that they are trusted, they are likely to be responsible for their actions and choices. This type of trust is built through transparent communication, where there is the setting of boundaries and expectations but with room for growth. It enables individuals to freely share their thoughts and ideas to create a culture of understanding and respect, and it strengthens the trust bond.

Responsibility is also a pillar of independence. Establishing responsibilities and roles that are challenging but respect their capability is important. Instilling in them responsibility for what they do develops the belief in accountability, which is one of the most precious qualities of independent individuals. This requires establishing goal-setting that is attainable and giving them the provision and support necessary for its attainment. As the individuals overcome these barriers, they gain a feeling of achievement and confidence in their capability.

Empowering individual independence is about giving people the means and skills required to make decisions and solve problems by themselves. This is done through training and learning, where people are stimulated to try in all manners and methods. Encouraging **problem-solving capability and critical thinking** makes it simpler for people to make independent decisions, lowering the necessity for information from outside.

Feedback is important in developing independence. Positive feedback helps individuals understand themselves and where they need to get better. Giving feedback in a positive, growth, and non-judgmental manner is important. It aids in building a culture of learning and growth where individuals feel motivated to improve.

Fostering a supportive environment is crucial in developing autonomy. This involves recognizing and encouraging achievements no matter how minor they are, and also encouraging failure. A supportive environment fosters resilience, which allows a person to endure adversity. Providing people with a choice to reflect on their experiences and learn from success and failure is also important.

Lastly, fostering independence is about making people responsible for their lives. It is about leading them to their full potential and equipping them with tools and support that allow them to succeed. By fostering a culture of responsibility, trust, and independence, people can acquire the confidence and capability to move through life and work on their own. As they mature, they come back not only to themselves but also to the organizations and communities they belong to.

A real-life example is Kohinoor, my son who is 13 years old, acquiring responsibility through trust and not through instruction.

📕 The Story of Kohinoor and the Unfinished Homework

Kohinoor had been struggling to complete his homework on time, often distracted by gadgets and shifting priorities. Instead of enforcing stricter rules or hovering over him, I decided to shift my approach. I told him,

"I trust you to manage your time. This is your responsibility. If you ever need help, I'm here."

At first, the delays continued. But gradually, he began setting his own reminders, organizing his study schedule, and completing assignments independently. One day, I noticed his planner filled with tasks he had created for himself. When I asked about it, he said with quiet confidence,

"I just wanted to show I can manage things my way."

That moment was a revelation—not about homework, but about **how empowerment begins when control is replaced by trust**. Giving him space allowed him to step into responsibility on his own terms.

Building Self-Esteem

Self-esteem is an essential component of personal growth and empowerment. It acts as a foundation upon which individuals can build confidence, resilience, and a sense of self-worth. Developing this crucial aspect of one's personality involves understanding the intricate relationship between self-perception and external influences.

At its core, self-esteem is shaped by an individual's belief in their own abilities and worthiness. This belief is often influenced by feedback from the environment, including interactions with family, peers, and societal norms. Positive reinforcement and supportive relationships play a significant role in fostering a healthy self-image. When individuals receive encouragement and recognition, they are more likely to perceive themselves as capable and valuable.

Conversely, negative feedback and criticism can undermine self- esteem, leading to self-doubt and a diminished sense of worth. The impact of such interactions can be profound, particularly if they occur during formative years. It is crucial to be mindful of the language and attitudes conveyed to others, as these can either uplift or diminish their self-perception.

Building self-esteem involves cultivating a mindset that emphasizes personal strengths and accomplishments. Recognizing and celebrating achievements, no matter how small, can reinforce a positive self-image. Setting realistic goals and acknowledging progress towards these goals also contribute to a sense of competence and self-efficacy.

Moreover, fostering self-esteem requires the development of self- compassion and the ability to forgive oneself for mistakes. Understanding that everyone experiences setbacks allows individuals to view failures as opportunities for growth rather than as reflections of inadequacy. This perspective encourages resilience and the willingness to try again, thus reinforcing self-esteem.

An important aspect of building self-esteem is the ability to assert oneself and establish boundaries. Assertiveness involves expressing one's needs and opinions confidently and respectfully. By doing so, individuals affirm their right to be heard and valued, which strengthens their sense of self-worth.

Creating an environment that supports the development of self- esteem is equally important. Surrounding oneself with positive influences, such as mentors, supportive friends, and communities that celebrate diversity and individuality, can reinforce a healthy self-image. These environments encourage individuals to embrace their uniqueness and contribute to a sense of belonging.

In educational settings, fostering self-esteem can be achieved through inclusive teaching practices that recognize and accommodate diverse learning styles and abilities. Encouraging participation, providing constructive feedback, and promoting collaboration can empower students to believe in their potential and develop self-confidence.

Ultimately, building self-esteem is a dynamic process that requires ongoing effort and reflection. By nurturing a positive self-image and embracing personal strengths, individuals can empower themselves to navigate life's challenges with confidence and resilience. This empowerment, in turn, enables them to contribute meaningfully to their communities and to lead fulfilling lives.

Empathy and Understanding

In the intricate tapestry of human interactions, the threads of empathy and understanding hold a unique position. They are not merely complementary skills but are foundational elements that define the quality of our relationships, both personal and professional. At the heart of empowerment lies the ability to truly connect with others, to perceive their emotions, and to comprehend their perspectives without judgment.

Empathy involves stepping into another person's shoes, seeing the world through their eyes, and feeling their emotions genuinely. It is a powerful tool that can transform interactions from superficial exchanges to meaningful dialogues. When individuals feel heard and understood, they are more likely to express themselves openly and engage more fully. This openness fosters an environment where ideas can be shared freely, and creativity can flourish.

Understanding, on the other hand, goes beyond empathy. It requires active listening and a conscious effort to grasp the underlying reasons behind a person's feelings and actions. Understanding is not about agreement, rather, it is about acknowledging the validity of another's experience, even if it differs from one's own. This acknowledgment is crucial in building trust and respect, essential components of any empowering relationship.

In the context of leadership and management, empathy and understanding are indispensable. Leaders who practice these skills can create a workplace culture that values diversity of thought and encourages collaboration. Such leaders are often seen as approachable and supportive, qualities that can inspire and motivate teams to achieve their best.

Moreover, empathy and understanding can significantly enhance conflict resolution. When disagreements arise, approaching them with an empathetic mindset can de-escalate tensions and lead to more constructive outcomes. By understanding the root causes of conflict and recognizing the emotions involved, parties can work towards solutions that satisfy all involved, rather than resorting to power struggles or coercion.

Practicing empathy and understanding requires self-awareness and patience. It involves setting aside preconceived notions and biases, allowing individuals to engage with others on a deeper level. This process can be challenging, especially in situations where emotions run high or when confronted with perspectives that starkly contrast with one's own. However, the rewards of cultivating these skills are manifold, leading to richer, more fulfilling interactions.

In educational settings, empathy and understanding are equally vital. Educators who employ these skills can better connect with students, creating a learning environment that is supportive and inclusive. By understanding the diverse backgrounds and challenges students face, educators can tailor their teaching approaches to meet individual needs, promoting a sense of belonging and engagement in the learning process.

Ultimately, the practice of empathy and understanding is a continuous journey of growth and learning. It encourages individuals to be more open-minded and compassionate, fostering a world where empowerment is the norm rather than the exception. By prioritizing these skills, individuals can contribute positively to their communities, enhancing both personal and collective well-being. In this way, empathy and understanding become not just tools for empowerment but essential elements of a thriving, interconnected society.

"Parenting is not about control—it's about creating space for children to find their own strength."

— Dr. Balvinder S. Banga

Chapter - 7
Workplace Empowerment

Creating Inclusive Cultures

In a high-speed organizational world today, creating a culture of inclusiveness is not just a matter of ethics, but it is a matter of strategy as well. Workplace empowerment is dependent on the ability of an organization to create a culture that makes every member feel valued, respected, and heard. These cultures do not come overnight but must be done consciously and repeatedly to break walls and build bridges between groups.

At the heart of creating inclusive cultures is the belief in diversity as strength. Businesses must go beyond numbers on diversity and commit to awareness and appreciation of the various perspectives that every employee contributes to the business. This entails not only seeing the obvious differences of race, gender, and age but also embracing ones like socioeconomic status, cognitive orientation, and life experience. Through this, businesses are able to tap the full potential of their human capital, driving innovation and growth.

Leadership has a significant role to play in shaping inclusive cultures. Leaders must model inclusion in their behavior and decision-making and set an example for others to follow. This includes listening to employees, open communication, and ensuring everyone's voice is heard and included. Furthermore, leadership must be committed to being transparent and accountable, openly addressing any instances of bias or discrimination and taking remedial measures where necessary.

Education and training are two of the most precious assets on the road to inclusivity. Organizations need to have robust training processes in place that educate employees about unconscious bias and equip them with the skills to facilitate inclusive engagement. They need to be dynamic and ongoing, responding to the fluid nature of the workforce and the needs of society. Sponsorship and mentorship schemes can also provide underrepresented groups with the excellent mentoring and sponsorship they require to map their career path and achieve their potential.

Practices and policies must be reviewed and reformed in order to remove structural barriers to inclusivity. That means looking to recruitment practices to make them equitable, creating career development that is inclusive of all, and creating flexible work arrangements that accommodate diverse needs. Organizations must also strive to create safe spaces where workers feel at ease to express their identities openly without fear of judgment or reprisal.

Employee resource groups (ERGs) can be excellent vehicles to build community and advance inclusion. ERGs enable employees to connect over common experiences and create change that benefits the organization at large. Organizational sponsorship of ERGs communicates that the organization is committed to inclusion and enables employees to be agents of change in workplace culture.

One of the clearest measures of an inclusive culture is not how many voices are present—but how many are truly heard. Sometimes, empowerment begins with one voice that dares to speak up. Here's how one junior employee reshaped a major system just by being given the space to contribute.

📘 Story: A Voice That Changed the Dashboard

A **Logistics company in Gurgaon**, monthly MIS reports were a pain point. The operations team relied on outdated, static dashboards that offered limited visibility into last-mile delivery accuracy. The IT team had long discussed revamping the system, but the suggestions usually came from senior developers or department heads.

During an internal feedback session, **Farheen**, a BI developer who had joined just six months ago, spoke up. She proposed integrating delivery-stage analytics using an alternative data model she had experimented with during a past internship.

Initially overlooked, her idea gained traction when a senior manager invited her to build a prototype as part of an internal **innovation challenge**. With mentoring support and two weeks of hands-on development, Farheen presented a live dashboard with real-time route deviation flags and predictive delivery windows.

The leadership team was impressed not only by the feature set, but by **how someone new, from a different cultural and educational background, had delivered a breakthrough solution**. That dashboard was adopted company-wide and is still a core part of Organization analytics stack.

Farheen was later nominated for a company-wide **Emerging Talent Award**. But more importantly, her story **reshaped how ideas were heard** at Company.

Farheen's breakthrough wasn't just a technical upgrade—it was a cultural shift. Her contribution reminded the leadership that innovation doesn't follow hierarchy; it follows empowerment. In response, her organization didn't just reward her idea— they institutionalized the practice of listening to every level of talent. This is the essence of inclusive empowerment: not just inviting people to the table, but ensuring their ideas are served.

Ultimately, the creation of inclusive cultures is a continuous process that requires dedication, reflection, and adaptation. It involves a collective effort from all members of an organization, driven by a shared vision of empowerment. By prioritizing inclusivity, organizations not only create a more equitable environment but also unlock the potential for greater creativity, collaboration, and success. In this way, they empower their workforce without overpowering individuals, fostering a culture where everyone can thrive.

Employee Autonomy

Organizations are finding the importance of giving employees a level of autonomy in their work increasingly valuable. Autonomy in the workplace means the amount of freedom and independence employees enjoy in their job tasks. It is not so much about giving employees the freedom to make decisions as about trusting them to get tasks done in a manner that is best for them and their strengths and working style.

Empowering employees gives them the authority to make decisions, and this makes them more willing and content in their job. This is because autonomy gives an individual a sense of responsibility and ownership. When individuals believe that they are responsible for what they are doing, they actually put in their time and energy, leading to high productivity and quality of work. By empowering employees to be responsible for their work, organizations are in a position to utilize the different skills and ideas that every individual within the team has to contribute.

Also, autonomy encourages creativity and innovation. In an environment where workers are not micromanaged, they can play around with new approaches and methods of accomplishing tasks without fearing immediate termination or rebuke. This can result in new problem-solving strategies and process innovations that would not have been discovered in a more managed environment. Encouraging an autonomy culture can assist in developing an innovative and forward-looking organizational culture.

But autonomy must be balanced. Autonomy can yield a range of positive results, but organizations need to have expectations in place and provide proper provision of resources and support. Employees need to have an idea of what their objectives are and where the limits are in which they can work. Feedback and communication are essential in ensuring employees remain aligned with the organization when working autonomously.

Leadership plays a very important part in creating an autonomous work environment. The leaders must create a culture of trust, communication, and encouragement. The leaders must empower the employees to express their ideas and concerns and create a culture where autonomy can grow. Training and development programs must be offered to the employees to empower them to learn skills that are essential to handle increased responsibilities.

It must also be remembered that not all people who work will be as comfortable or as capable with independence. There are some individuals who will be more comfortable with and better suited with more rules and structure in the workplace. Companies must be willing and compassionate towards individuals' needs and capabilities and offer different amounts of autonomy based on what is optimal for the employee and company.

Employee autonomy, simply put, is not relinquishing control but creating a balanced culture in which employees are encouraged to take the initiative. Not just good for the employee in terms of job satisfaction and career opportunities, but also the organization as a whole and its achievement and adaptability. **Proper application of autonomy can enable organizations to create an**

empowered, creative, and robust set of individuals who are capable of coping with the complexity of today's rapidly changing business environment.

Professional Development

In the hectic working life of today, professional growth is the solution to personal and organizational growth. It is not just acquiring new skills and knowledge but a holistic approach towards creating an environment where the employees are empowered, valued, and encouraged to perform to their potential.

Professional development begins with the discovery of the individual talent and aspirations of each member of the labor force. Each one has a different talent and potential, and these must be identified. The managers play a major role in identifying these strengths and aligning them with challenges that motivate the employees to grow. This alignment not only leads to individual development but also propels the organization forward with innovation and creativity.

Continual learning is a broad dimension of successful professional development. The speed of today's changing world requires staying current with industry trends, technologies, and methods. Learning organizations are those that create a culture of curiosity and experimentation. Provision of workshops, courses, seminars, and other learning avenues makes a company ensure that its employees are competitive and flexible.

Mentorship also constitutes an important part of the professional development framework. A good mentorship program will significantly enhance the learning experience by exposing workers to skilled peers who will mentor and advise them. Mentors share advice, anecdotal experiences, and navigate mentees through difficulty. Apart from fostering a sense of belongingness and ownership, it also helps to transfer knowledge and organizational culture.

Setting precise, measurable goals is at the center of successful professional development. Goals provide direction and focus, enabling one to concentrate efforts on concrete outcomes. These types of goals must be aligned with personal goals and firm goals to provide a consistent direction. Review and feedback must also be maintained to track development, recognize accomplishments, and identify areas of improvement.

Furthermore, professional development is not a one-size-fits-all solution. Developing tailored plans to address distinct interests and employee needs can lead to greater and more effective development. Development plans for individuals account for variability in learning styles, career aspirations, and existing skills and provide a personal path to success.

The role of leadership in professional growth cannot be overstated. Leaders must be learning and growth oriented, with emphasis on the importance of continuous improvement. Through an open and positive workplace, leaders are able to enable their organizations to own their own growth processes individually. This empowerment results in higher job satisfaction, better retention, and an incredibly engaged employee base.

In essence, professional development is a dynamic and ongoing process that requires commitment on the part of employees and organizations. It is a question of creating opportunities, nurturing talent, and a culture that not only supports growth but demands it. By investing in the professional development of their employees, organizations not only increase their competitive edge but also foster overall organizational health and employee job satisfaction. This reciprocal reliance of organizational performance on individual development makes it imperative to empower and not control workers in the workplace.

Recognition and Reward

Reward and recognition are the very pillars of leadership and management that give rise to **a culture of motivation and growth**. These are not to be taken lightly, for they give rise to a culture in which the members of the team feel valued and encouraged to deliver their best. Reward and recognition are not just about rewarding the task, but more about rewarding the journey, the effort, and the innovation that the people put in.

Recognition, in fact, is all about recognizing individual contributions of teammates. It may be in the form of many different types, from a simple oral appreciation during a meeting to a more formal system of recognition. The key is to ensure that recognition is timely, specific, and genuine. When individuals feel appreciated and recognized for their contributions, it gives them a sense of belongingness and commitment to the organization. It reminds them that their hard work is not going to waste and that their contributions are vital to the success of the team.

Reward, on the other hand, will likely encompass material rewards that are offered for higher performance or achievement. These could be as commonplace as promotions and bonuses or more creative rewards such as more days off or experience-based rewards. Effective reward systems are those that align with organizational values and goals and personalized incentives of the workers. Rewards are needed to be perceived as equitable and available, in order that they will be motivating and not divisive.

An effective reward and recognition system is one that has a deep understanding of what drives each and every individual on their team. It is hearing their dreams, understanding their capabilities, and celebrating their achievements in a manner that is most personal to them. The best managers at it are those who have open lines of communication, and give feedback and dialogue that allow them to tailor their reward and recognition systems to the very particular needs of their team.

In addition to individual motivation, the power of reward and appreciation has a broader impact on the team. It fosters a culture of excellence in the team, where the members are motivated to complement and appreciate each other's success. It generates a positive feedback mechanism, where appreciation of an individual's effort motivates others to work towards the same, thereby enhancing the performance of the team.

It is also important to mention that good reward and recognition systems are responsive and dynamic. As organizations change, the reward and recognition practices also need to change. This is through constant review of dominant practices and being open to make changes when needed. By being sensitive to changing needs and motivations of their people, leaders can make their reward and recognition programs effective and meaningful.

Finally, reward and recognition are not only morale-sustaining or performance-promoting, but it is about instilling a culture of respect, trust, and appreciation. When the employees are made to feel that they are truly valued and rewarded for their work, they are likely to stay committed, motivated, and dedicated to organizational achievement. Recognition and reward thus become powerful tools of empowering individuals and organizational achievement.

COMMUNITY EMPOWERMENT

Dr. Balvinder S Banga

"Communities rise when their members feel seen, heard, and capable of change."

— Dr. Balvinder S. Banga

Chapter - 8

Pulse Of Change- Empowering Communities to Lead

Grassroots Movements

Grassroots movements, by definition typically emerging from society's periphery, have long been a force shaping social, political, and cultural formations. Grassroots movements by definition are characterized by being bottom-up in orientation, with change being generated by the self-activity of individuals and communities and not by top-down intervention by established institutions. The power of grassroots movements lies in the fact that they have the ability to empower ordinary people, give them a voice and platform to express opposition to change.

Underlying grass roots movements is the philosophy of collective action. This is premised on the belief that individuals united by a common purpose have the ability to command a great deal of power and bring about change. Unlike hierarchical models, grass roots movements are frequently decentralized and depend on the involvement and input of a large number of people. This type of organization is conducive to a perception of ownership and empowerment of the stakeholders since they are motivated to contribute actively towards the objectives of the movement.

One of the defining features of grassroots movements is that they are resilient and adaptable. Grassroots movements are apt to be found in response to specific social or political concerns, e.g., those concerning civil rights, the environment, or economic inequality. The ability of these movements to mobilize quickly and adapt based on the events unfolding is what gives them authority and potency at their causes. Grassroots movements have a tendency to use the power of storytelling, utilizing personal experience to bring attention to the impact of systemic issues and build support among a broader base.

The contribution of technology to grassroots movements cannot be exaggerated. The advent of the digital era has made social media and internet networks great mobilization and awareness platforms. The platforms provide grassroots movements with a worldwide voice, irrespective of location, and unite like-minded people across the globe. The viral capabilities of social media allow the movements to go viral and gain popularity within a short time, giving them a public voice and a perception of solidarity among their followers.

Grassroots movements, however great their potential, are also faced with many challenges. Grassroots movements lack resources and can struggle to muster momentum in the long run. The very decentralization of such movements, which is so empowering, can also cause fragmentation and strategic incoherence. Grassroots movements can face opposition from entrenched institutions and attempts at co-optation or sabotage of their efforts.

To overcome these challenges, social movements must emphasize openness and collaboration. Alliances with other movements and organizations can possibly make them stronger and open doors to more resources and knowledge. Furthermore, developing an open and respectful dialogue culture within the movement can make it easier to resolve internal conflicts and bring more diverse voices and perspectives to the forefront to be heard and respected.

Lastly, the effectiveness of people's movements lies in their ability to inspire and mobilize individuals to act as one. By making citizens speak up for change and challenging vested power, people's movements are a testament to the power of change of the common people. Through their determination to seek justice and equality, the people's movements remind us that significant change tends to begin at the grassroots level with people coming together to envision and create a better world.

Building Community Leaders

In the intricate tapestry of societal progress, community leaders play an indispensable role. They are the catalysts for change, the visionaries who inspire and mobilize others towards collective goals. Understanding the essence of nurturing such leaders forms a cornerstone in the broader framework of empowerment. These individuals, often emerging from grassroots levels, possess the potential to influence, guide, and transform their communities effectively.

The process of building community leaders begins with recognizing and cultivating intrinsic qualities such as empathy, resilience, and integrity. These traits are the bedrock upon which effective leadership is constructed. Empathy enables leaders to connect with their community on a profound level, understanding their needs and aspirations. Resilience ensures that they can withstand challenges and setbacks, maintaining momentum in the face of adversity. Integrity fosters trust, an essential component for any leader seeking to galvanize a community.

A critical aspect of developing community leaders lies in providing them with the necessary tools and resources. This involves offering training programs focused on leadership skills, conflict resolution, and strategic planning. Such educational initiatives equip potential leaders with the knowledge and confidence required to navigate complex social dynamics. Moreover, mentorship from seasoned leaders can provide invaluable insights and guidance, aiding in the practical application of these skills.

Equally important is the creation of platforms for these emerging leaders to voice their ideas and initiatives. Community forums, workshops, and local councils serve as arenas where they can engage with broader audiences, refine their communication skills, and gather support for their projects. Encouraging participation in these settings not only aids in personal development but also strengthens community bonds by fostering a culture of inclusivity and collaboration.

Moreover, fostering a supportive environment is crucial in the journey of building community leaders. This involves creating a culture that celebrates diversity and encourages innovation. By embracing different perspectives and approaches, communities can harness a wider range of solutions to address their unique challenges. Support networks, including peer groups and community organizations, can provide the encouragement and reinforcement necessary for leaders to thrive.

Empowerment also involves recognizing the significance of accountability. Community leaders must be held to high standards, ensuring that their actions align with the values and needs of the communities they serve. Establishing transparent systems for feedback and evaluation helps maintain this accountability, fostering a sense of responsibility and commitment among leaders.

Ultimately, the goal of building community leaders is not merely to enhance individual capabilities but to create a ripple effect that benefits the entire community. As these leaders grow and evolve, they inspire others to step forward, perpetuating a cycle of empowerment and positive change. By investing in the development of community leaders, societies can cultivate a robust foundation for sustainable progress, driven by individuals who are equipped to lead with compassion, wisdom, and integrity.

Community leadership often doesn't begin with big speeches or lofty plans. Sometimes, it begins with a simple decision—to take action. This is the story of how one small effort turned into a wave of empowerment and connection in my own neighborhood.

Story: Reviving a Park, Reviving a Community

Empowerment often begins not with a grand plan—but with a quiet decision to act. In the heart of our busy society in **Gurgaon**, our park—once filled with laughter, morning walks, and the hum of everyday life—had slowly slipped into neglect. What was once a vibrant community space had become overgrown, littered, and forgotten.

Moved by its decline, **I decided to lead a quiet transformation**. Instead of waiting for official action, I chose to begin with what I had—time, intention, and a belief in people. With gentle conversations, I began involving our neighbors. **My wife, Ritu**, brought women together over tea to share the idea. **Our sons,**

Mansidak and Kohinoor, designed a simple digital campaign

"Let's Bring Our Park Back."

What followed was inspiring. Weekends became community days **cleaning, planting trees, repainting walls**. Children created art that spoke of hope and unity. A nearby vendor supported us with solar lights, bringing warmth and safety to our evenings.

In just a few months, the park transformed—not just physically, but emotionally. It became a shared space of pride, participation, and purpose.

This was more than just reviving a park—it was about **reviving connection**, **ownership**, and **the spirit of empowerment from within.**

*What began as a humble clean-up effort blossomed into a deeply transformative act of community ownership? This journey reaffirmed a simple truth- **empowerment is contagious.** When one person steps forward with conviction, others find the courage to follow and in doing so, the community itself is reborn. True grassroots* *leadership is not about position, it's about purpose and participation*

Resource Allocation

The fine art of organizational management involves resource allocation as a crucial element. At the core of every thriving business is the ability to allocate resources in such a way that each element of the organization is able to meet its goals. This activity, while seeming so straightforward, requires a refined appreciation of both short-term needs and long-term aspirations.

The first step in the efficient utilization of resources is to know the resources present at hand. This includes not only funds but also individuals, technology, and time. All these resources are the core of the functioning of an organization, and their value can differ based on the context in which they are being used. Therefore, the entire gamut of resources present at hand needs to be considered.

Once resources are identified, the key to the next step is prioritization. Organizations must go through their strategic goals, determining the projects that bring the greatest return to them. That means careful analysis of potential return on investment and the risk involved in different projects. There must be a prioritization order to be clearly understood so that resources are allocated to activities that fit the organizational mission and have high potential gains.

But allocation is not a sporadic decision but a continuous process. It needs continuous monitoring and rebalancing.

Circumstances external to the firm, including the forces of the market, economic changes, and technological advances, can suddenly change the conditions in which a firm is operating. Within the firm, project advancement and changes in employee needs can also necessitate balancing of resources. With a flexible approach, organizations are able to respond fast to such changes, minimizing disruptions while maximizing productivity.

The core of this flexibility is the participation of the stakeholders at all tiers. Communication that is open ensures that all understand the justification of the allocation decision and can give good feedback. If the decision-making process involves the team members, they will be able to commit to the result and support the organization in attaining its objective.

In addition, technology has a revolutionary impact on resource distribution. Since sophisticated analytics software is now accessible, organizations are able to forecast requirements with more accuracy, map inefficiency, and allocate resources more optimally. Data-driven insights enable better decision-making, minimizing wastage and maximizing productivity.

But even with advanced equipment, the human element cannot be done away with. Successful utilization of resources also hinges on the capacity of leadership to motivate and inspire. Leaders who empower their employees give the type of environment where workers feel valued and trusted, and are motivated to use resources effectively and innovate as needed.

Lastly, effective resource allocation is all about balance. It is a delicate balancing of short-term necessities against long-term aspirations, and quantitative information against qualitative views. Effective resource allocation, when executed well, not only sustains the business, but also sets the stage for long-term expansion.

In an ever-evolving business environment, organizations that master the art of their assets achieve competitive advantage. Connecting their assets to strategic goals positions them to not just survive but flourish, turn adversity into opportunity, and foster long-term success. Empowerment, thus, is not so much about assets but about assets being used to drive innovation and growth..

Sustainable Development

Sustainable The phrase "**Sustainable Development**" has been very much in vogue over the last few years. It describes the situation that whatever we do now must not damage the ability of yet unborn generations to meet their own needs, in addition to demanding compatibility of economic development, social justice, and protection of the environment. This strategy aims to address the interconnections between **poverty, injustice, and environmental degradation**. Sustainable development is all about achieving a balance between **economic, social, and environmental objectives** so that the world is a better and more equitable and sustainable world. Economic growth seeks to enhance livelihoods and bridge gaps as well as expand. This includes investing in education and skills to make the labor market more inclusive, as well as innovation, entrepreneurship, and small and medium-sized enterprises.

Socially, sustainable development aims to eliminate poverty and inequality and empower the poor and vulnerable. It entails ensuring access to basic services like social protection, healthcare, and education. It entails providing equal opportunity to everyone regardless of age, ethnicity, or origin. Sustainable development aims to ensure harmonious societies where everyone can enjoy high levels of living by ensuring social realities become a reality.

Environmental significance is the protection of natural resources and encouraging moral consumption and production habits. It entails decreasing the environmental impact of individuals and companies, minimizing waste, and changing from fossil fuels to clean energy. To maintain the earth's ecosystem balance, it entails maintaining ecosystems and biodiversity.

Cooperation and partnership between sectors and levels of society are necessary in the implementation of sustainable development. Governments, businesses, and civil society actors need to collaborate in developing laws and procedures which will enhance long-term success. It involves spurring technological transfer and innovation and raising funds to finance costs for sustainable operations.

Education and awareness creation are also important elements of sustainable development. People can make the world sustainable by making the world conscious of the necessity for sustainable living and encouraging people to live sustainably. This entails educating the masses on the impact of their actions and empowering them to make decisions that will benefit the world and generations to come.

Despite the challenges, there is an opportunity to redefine prosperity and progress through this shift to sustainable development. The aspirations and hopes of today and tomorrow can be realized in a more equitable, sustainable, and efficient world if long-term sustainability takes precedence over short-term gains. This new way opens to a better, more sustainable world for everyone through the demanding of commitment to transformation, imagination, and cooperation.

EMPOWERMENT THROUGH TECHNOLOGY

"Information is not power until it's accessible, inclusive, and wisely used."

— Dr. Balvinder S. Banga

Chapter - 9
Digital Empowerment & Ethical Innovation

Access to Information

Though it is the central right to empower individuals and communities in the information era, it is the foundation of informed **decision-making, democratic engagement, and sustainable development**. By providing individuals with a setting where information becomes accessible, societies can promote transparency, accountability, and development.

The principle of access to information relies on the assumption that all individuals are entitled to receive, access, and share information. It is a condition precedent to the enjoyment of other freedoms and rights since it equips citizens with the ability to criticize the authorities, participate in civic affairs, and be capable of holding the authorities accountable. Access to information without charge reduces domination between the rulers and the ruled and hence makes society more equitable.

Technological revolution has, in effect, changed the very face of information availability. The internet, more specifically, has transformed the way information is disseminated and consumed. It provides unrivaled access to information opportunities from a wide range of information sources anywhere on the globe.

This global interconnectedness has provided access to knowledge, breaking down barriers that earlier restricted knowledge flow.

But the digital divide still exists. Advances in technology have placed information in the hands of many, but they have also revealed the gaps between digital haves and have-nots. These need to be bridged in a way that makes access to information ubiquitous in real terms. Every effort must be made to bring digital literacy classes and low-cost internet connectivity to marginalized population to not further expand existing gaps.

Furthermore, the **quality and honesty** of information posted online can be extremely variable. With the age of "fake news" and disinformation, the critical thinking skill is more urgently needed than ever before. People need to be educated with the skill of distinguishing between credible and non-credible sources. **Media literacy** instruction can go a long way in teaching the public how to assess the truthfulness and reliability of information.

Governments and institutions have to play their part in making information available by passing and implementing legislation that will promote openness and transparency. This involves passing freedom of information acts that allow citizens to request information in the possession of public authorities. Freedom of information acts are a valuable tool in the fight against corruption and in establishing trust between citizens and the state.

Further, information accessibility must be inclusive, targeting all segments of society, including the marginalized. Information must be made available in multiple languages and accessible media to cater to the disabled. Inclusiveness benefits individuals and also increases society's overall knowledge pool.

In summary, access to information is the foundation of empowerment. ***Through access to information, individuals are able to make informed choices, contribute effectively to society, and participate in the democratic process***. By making access to information the priority, societies can unlock the potential of their citizens and power innovation and development. The trick is to make this access inclusive, trustworthy, and equitable and thus create a more informed and empowered world.

Digital Literacy

In an era where technology permeates every facet of our lives, digital literacy emerges as an essential skill set that empowers individuals to navigate the vast digital landscape with confidence and discernment. This chapter delves into the multifaceted nature of digital literacy, exploring its significance, components, and the role it plays in fostering an empowered society.

At its core, digital literacy encompasses the ability to effectively and critically engage with digital technologies and platforms. It extends beyond mere technical proficiency to include a comprehensive understanding of how to use digital tools responsibly and ethically. This involves not only the skills to operate devices and software but also the capacity to evaluate information, communicate effectively, and participate actively in digital environments.

One of the primary components of digital literacy is the ability to discern credible information from misinformation. In a world where information is abundant and easily accessible, the challenge lies in sifting through the noise to identify reliable sources. Critical thinking and analytical skills are paramount in assessing the validity of online content, and these skills form the cornerstone of digital literacy. By fostering these abilities, individuals are better equipped to make informed decisions and contribute meaningfully to digital discourse.

Communication in the digital realm is another vital aspect of digital literacy. With the proliferation of social media and digital communication platforms, the ability to convey ideas clearly and respectfully is crucial. Digital literacy encompasses understanding the nuances of online communication, including tone, context, and cultural sensitivity. It involves recognizing the impact of digital footprints and the importance of maintaining a positive online presence.

Moreover, digital literacy entails a deep understanding of digital rights and responsibilities. Awareness of privacy issues, data protection, and cybersecurity is essential in safeguarding personal information and respecting the rights of others. This knowledge empowers individuals to navigate digital spaces safely and responsibly, fostering a culture of respect and accountability.

Digital literacy also plays a pivotal role in promoting inclusivity and bridging the digital divide. By ensuring that individuals from diverse backgrounds have access to digital tools and resources, digital literacy initiatives can help level the playing field and provide equal opportunities for learning and growth. This inclusivity is vital in fostering a society where everyone can participate fully in the digital world, regardless of socioeconomic status or geographic location.

In educational settings, integrating digital literacy into the curriculum equips students with the skills they need to thrive in an increasingly digital world. Educators play a crucial role in nurturing digital literacy by creating environments that encourage exploration, creativity, and critical thinking. By doing so, they prepare students not only for academic success but also for lifelong learning and adaptability in a rapidly changing technological landscape.

Ultimately, digital literacy is not a static skill set but a dynamic and evolving competency. As technology continues to advance, so too must our understanding and application of digital literacy. By embracing a culture of continuous learning and adaptation, individuals can harness the power of digital technologies to enhance their personal and professional lives, contributing to a more empowered and informed society.

Social Media Influence

In today's interconnected world, social media platforms have emerged as powerful tools that shape opinions, behaviors, and cultures. The impact of these platforms transcends geographical boundaries, enabling individuals to share their thoughts, experiences, and creativity with a global audience. While this digital connectivity offers numerous opportunities for empowerment, it also presents challenges that require careful navigation.

Social media's influence is profound in its ability to amplify voices and democratize information dissemination. Individuals who may have felt marginalized or voiceless in traditional media landscapes now find platforms to express themselves and rally support for causes they are passionate about. This democratization fosters a sense of community and belonging among users, encouraging them to participate actively in societal conversations. The accessibility of social media allows for diverse perspectives to be shared, challenging dominant narratives and promoting inclusivity.

However, the influence of social media is not without its complexities. The algorithms that govern these platforms often prioritize content that is sensational or emotionally charged, which can skew perceptions and amplify misinformation. Users may find themselves in echo chambers, where their existing beliefs are reinforced rather than challenged, leading to polarization and the erosion of constructive dialogue. This phenomenon underscores the importance of media literacy, equipping users with the skills to critically evaluate the information they encounter and engage thoughtfully with differing viewpoints.

Moreover, the curated nature of social media content can create unrealistic standards and expectations. The constant exposure to idealized versions of life can impact mental health, leading to feelings of inadequacy or anxiety. It is crucial for individuals to cultivate a balanced relationship with these platforms, recognizing the difference between curated content and reality. Encouraging self-awareness and mindfulness in social media consumption can help mitigate these negative effects, fostering a healthier digital environment.

The role of influencers further illustrates the dual nature of social media's impact. Influencers wield significant power in shaping consumer behavior and cultural trends. Their endorsements can boost a brand's visibility or promote social causes. However, the authenticity of these endorsements is often questioned, as commercial interests may drive influencer content. Consumers must remain vigilant, discerning genuine advocacy from marketing strategies, and influencers themselves bear the responsibility of maintaining transparency and integrity in their engagements.

Educational institutions and organizations play a pivotal role in shaping the discourse around social media influence. By integrating digital literacy into curricula, they empower individuals to navigate these platforms responsibly, fostering a generation that is both informed and critical. Workshops, seminars, and discussions can further enhance understanding, equipping users with the tools to harness social media's potential for positive impact while mitigating its pitfalls.

Social media, when leveraged thoughtfully, can be a catalyst for empowerment. It offers a platform for advocacy, creativity, and connection, bridging gaps and fostering understanding among diverse communities. By approaching social media with a critical eye and a mindful attitude, users can transform it from a source of potential overwhelm into a powerful tool for personal and collective growth. The challenge lies in maintaining this balance, ensuring that the influence of social media enhances rather than overpowers the individual's agency and autonomy.

Bridging the Digital Divide

In the contemporary landscape of technological advancement, the digital divide remains a formidable barrier that separates those with access to information technology from those without. This gap is not merely about the presence or absence of technology, it encompasses the broader issues of accessibility, affordability, and digital literacy. Addressing these factors is crucial to empowering communities rather than overpowering them with the rapid pace of digital evolution.

The digital divide is often most pronounced in marginalized communities, where socio-economic factors hinder access to essential technological resources. This disparity can lead to significant disadvantages in education, employment, and access to information. To bridge this divide, a multifaceted approach is required, focusing on infrastructure, education, and policy reforms.

In discussions about digital inclusion, we often focus on infrastructure, policies, or devices but the most compelling stories come from individuals whose lives transform because of access. To illustrate how ethical digital empowerment can change trajectories, consider the journey of Meera, a rural woman in eastern India who turned connectivity into community growth.

📖 Story: "From Isolation to Innovation: A Rural Woman's Digital Journey"

In the remote village of Kachipur, nestled amidst the hills of eastern India, lived Meera, a 35-year-old mother of two. With limited access to resources and opportunities, Meera's days were confined to household chores and tending to a small patch of farmland.

The turning point came when a local non-profit organization introduced a digital literacy program in the village. Skeptical yet curious, Meera enrolled in the program. Over weeks, she learned to operate a smartphone, navigate the internet, and understand basic digital tools.

Empowered with new skills, Meera began exploring online platforms to sell her handcrafted bamboo products. She joined e- commerce sites, promoted her items on social media, and connected with customers beyond her village. Orders started pouring in, and Meera's modest venture transformed into a thriving business.

Recognizing the potential, she collaborated with the non-profit to train other women in the village, creating a community of digitally empowered entrepreneurs.

Meera's journey is a powerful reminder that digital empowerment is not just about technology it's about trust, relevance, and access delivered ethically. When innovation is grounded in empathy and community need, it doesn't just bridge a digital divide—it builds pathways to opportunity. Her story invites us to ask!

Building up infrastructure is the most important step in reducing the digital gap. Making sure that underserved communities have access to high-speed internet and contemporary communication technology is a basic step. This means not only building things like cables and satellites, but also making sure that low-income families can afford these services. The government and the private sector need to work together to lower costs and build the infrastructure that will make it easier for everyone to get to.

Education is very important for giving people the skills they need to use digital technologies to their full potential. Digital literacy programs should be a part of all stages of education, from elementary school to adult learning centers. These programs should focus on teaching important skills including how to use digital tools, how to stay secure online, and how to solve problems in a digital setting. By doing this, people aren't just passive users of technology; they're also active participants in the digital world.

Policy changes are necessary to make the digital gap smaller. Policymakers need to make laws that promote digital equality their top priority. These laws should make sure that everyone has the right to access information and digital tools. This means giving firms reasons to make technologies that work for a wide range of people and making sure that rules are followed that stop companies from controlling all digital resources.

Also, creating a culture of diversity and inclusion in the tech business can lead to new ideas that help populations that aren't getting enough help. When a lot of different people work together to make digital tools, they're more likely to come up with solutions that work for a wider range of people.

The digital gap is a big problem, but it also opens up new ways to grow and come up with new ideas. When societies face these problems with empathy and a dedication to inclusivity, they may make places where technology is a bridge instead of a barrier. This effort needs public and commercial partnerships, community projects, and working together with other countries.

The end goal is to give people and communities the tools they need to fully participate in the digital age. People are empowered not just by giving them access, but by creating an atmosphere where they can use technology to make their lives better and make a real difference in society.

If we deal with the core causes of the digital divide and put in place smart solutions, we can get closer to a future where technology is a way to empower people instead of a way to divide them.

Respecting culture is not just tolerance—it's inclusion, celebration, and empowerment."

— Dr. Balvinder S. Banga

Chapter - 10

Cultural Empowerment

Celebrating Diversity

In order to create a peaceful setting that fosters empowerment and not control, one needs to understand that diversity is complex. Diversity involves a very large amount of things when it comes to people, for instance, their race, gender, age, religion, handicap, and sexual orientation. In creating society and the workplace where everyone feels valued and respected, one needs to observe and value these differences.

Diversity is worth it since it gives us so many different viewpoints to enrich our lives. Each person has his/her own experience, cultural understanding, and conviction that allows us all to perceive the world more completely. All these viewpoints put together might give us new ideas and innovative solutions to problems. Diverse groups work better than non-diverse groups because they disrupt the current state of affairs and innovate.

And respect for diversity is not so much about noticing differences as it is about striving to understand and accept them. That involves creating space for individuals to feel comfortable speaking their mind without fear and being themselves. There is some work to be done to eliminate stereotypes and prejudices that might get in the way of real understanding. In our practice, we make space for respect and working together, where differences are not only accepted but valued.

Diversity is most critical in leveling the playing field as far as empowerment is concerned. Individuals who would otherwise be disenfranchised or marginalized can be empowered through diversity of thought in decision-making. Diversity ensures all interests and concerns are heard and results in more equitable outcomes. We empower individuals to drive their own responsibilities and assist us in achieving shared goals by respecting differing thoughts.

In addition, education and leadership diversity must be welcomed. In schools, many different subjects that encompass numerous cultures and history can enable students to study the world in an integrated fashion. This is something that enables students to be more tolerant and compassionate, and this will enable them to be more adaptable to an increasingly globalized world. Similarly, leaders who are all about diversity and inclusion are more capable of leading companies to sustainable success. They build environments where new ideas can flourish and every member of the team can feel that their diverse contributions matter.

But to truly embrace diversity, you must also accept and address problems that accompany it. When people disagree, there can be disagreement, but these are learning and growth opportunities. People can agree on some things and make their societies more integrated and resilient by being receptive to other ideas and willing to listen when there is a problem.

Lastly, celebrating diversity is an ongoing process that needs to be done with intention and commitment. It is all about valuing the dignity of every human being and putting in place processes that enable them to grow and thrive. By creating a platform where diversity is valued, we empower individuals with the means to realize their potential, contribute positively to society, and create a future where differences are valued and celebrated as the source of our strength.

One wonderful example- Multicultural Team Solving a Local Water Crisis

In one of those small communities where pure water was running low, a task force was formed made up of people from different walks of life a retired farm worker, a young engineer, a school teacher, and a disabled woman who depended on a community well. They did not argue. Initially, they differed. They emphasized traditional practices, the engineer noticed solar filtration, and the teacher promoted water education in schools. But they did not argue.

Then they combined ideas -

Leveraged the farmer's local knowledge regarding underground sources, Installed the engineer's solar-powered filter, and included the teacher's water-saving curriculum in schools.

This was a participatory process that resulted in a sustainable solution. The disabled woman made sure that the new system was inclusive to all.

Moral: Diversity did not hold them back—it created a more practical, inclusive, and sustainable solution.

Preserving Heritage

The need to maintain cultural heritage tends to arise as a major issue in the dynamic balance between tradition and development. The values, customs, artifacts, and beliefs that characterize a society are all part of its cultural heritage. It is a foundation upon which the next generation will build and, at the same time, a bridge linking the past to the future. During a time of accelerated technological progress and globalization, it is important to maintain those traditions.

The first step towards attributing the value of cultural heritage is to acknowledge the manner in which it ties us together in a sense of identity and belongingness. The worldview and pride that a person has are influenced by the framework that is provided by tradition, customs, and history. Since it provides continuity in the midst of change, such inherent value is fundamental to the sustenance of the social fabric. Conservation of heritage ensures that cultural change is established on a rich tapestry of common knowledge and experience.

Additionally, **cultural heritage is one of the fundamental reasons why human experience is rich**. By providing alternative insights and solutions to problems, it makes societies richer. Societies can acquire various knowledge and traditions that would be otherwise lost by holding on to various customs. Because it promotes the merging of ideas and traditions from various cultures, diversity promotes creativity and innovation.

The second key consideration is the economic value of heritage preservation. Heritage has the potential to contribute significantly to economic development, especially in the tourism sector. Cultural events, cultural practices, and historical places attract tourists to visit, hence boosting the economy. Economic development can be promoted without compromising the identity of communities by investing in the preservation of such heritage properties.

It is impossible to turn a blind eye to issues of preservation of heritage in the face of modernization. Traditional lifestyles are normally vulnerable to urbanization, industrialization, and the homogenization of world culture. The issues, however, also open up the possibility of the development of new mechanisms of preservation of heritage. For example, digital technology offers a platform for bringing cultural practices into the public domain through new documentation and sharing practices.

Societies can innovate in preserving and presenting their heritage in digital repositories, augmented reality, and virtual reality.

Education has a significant function in the preservation of cultural heritage. Kids can be educated about honoring their heritage at a young age through the inclusion of cultural studies in schools. To make sure that cultural norms are not only remembered but also practiced and implemented, education incorporates an obligation to preserve and propagate them.

It is critical that the preservation initiatives involve the local populations. Giving people a sense of pride and ownership through community-led initiatives works towards empowering people to claim their cultural heritage. Joint initiatives by communities, organizations, and governments can create sustainable preservation models that are respectful of tradition but also address the needs of the present.

The purpose of preserving the cultural heritage is to accept change prudently and not resist it so that the progress is respectful towards the past. Societies can navigate the challenges of the modern world and hold on to their heritage by valuing and investing in it. **A tolerant and peaceful world has to balance preserving tradition with accepting innovation.**

Sometimes, cultural empowerment begins with the smallest gestures—those that connect generations and restore pride in one's roots.

📘 My Friend Meera's Grandy and the Dupatta of Dreams.

When Meera was assigned a school project on "What makes you proud?", she struggled. Born in an urban Indian suburb, her daily life was filled with smartphones and pizza, not rituals and stories.

That evening, she asked her grandmother, Nani, what made her proud. Without saying a word, Nani brought out an old trunk. Inside was a brightly colored **phulkari dupatta**, hand-embroidered by Nani's mother when she was a girl in Punjab.

As Nani unfolded the dupatta, she told Meera how each pattern had meaning—courage, resilience, fertility. She shared how women gathered to sing, sew, and tell stories, passing down not just cloth, but wisdom.

Inspired, Meera wore the dupatta for her school presentation. She shared its story, not as something old and dusty, but as something **alive**, woven with love, pain, and history. Her classmates listened quietly, and her teacher teared up.

For Meera, it wasn't just a grade. It was a realization: her culture wasn't behind her. It was a strength she could carry forward.

Meera's story reminds us that cultural empowerment doesn't always require grand initiatives. Sometimes, it's about rediscovering the beauty in our own family stories and feeling proud to carry them forward. When the past becomes part of our present identity, it empowers us with purpose, pride, and belonging.

Cultural Exchange

In the intricate tapestry of human interactions, cultural exchange emerges as a dynamic thread, weaving diverse narratives into a cohesive whole. It is through the sharing and acceptance of different cultural practices, beliefs, and values that societies can truly empower one another. This process not only enriches individual lives but also fosters a collective understanding that transcends geographical boundaries.

Cultural exchange operates on multiple levels, from the individual to the community, and extends to the global stage. At its core, it involves the mutual sharing of customs, traditions, languages, and arts. This exchange can take the form of academic exchanges, international festivals, culinary experiences, or even through digital communication platforms that connect people across continents.

One of the most profound impacts of cultural exchange is its ability to challenge preconceived notions and stereotypes. When individuals are exposed to different ways of life, they begin to question their assumptions and broaden their perspectives. This openness to new ideas is a critical component of empowerment, as it encourages individuals to think critically and empathetically about the world around them.

Moreover, cultural exchange nurtures creativity and innovation. By integrating diverse cultural elements, individuals and communities can develop unique solutions to common challenges. The fusion of different artistic styles, for instance, can lead to the creation of new art forms that resonate with a wider audience. Similarly, in business, understanding and incorporating diverse cultural practices can lead to more effective communication strategies and product designs.

In educational contexts, cultural exchange plays a pivotal role in shaping global citizens. Students who engage with peers from different cultural backgrounds gain invaluable insights into global issues and develop skills that are essential in a multicultural world. These experiences foster a sense of global responsibility and prepare individuals to contribute positively to international communities.

However, for cultural exchange to be truly empowering, it must be approached with sensitivity and respect. It is essential to recognize the power dynamics that can exist in these interactions and strive to create a balance that honors all cultures involved. This means actively listening, learning, and adapting, rather than imposing one's own cultural norms onto others.

Technology has become an indispensable tool in facilitating cultural exchange. Social media platforms, virtual reality experiences, and online forums provide unprecedented opportunities for individuals to connect and share their cultures. These digital spaces can serve as bridges, bringing people closer together and fostering a sense of shared humanity.

Yet, it is crucial to remain mindful of the potential pitfalls of cultural appropriation, where elements of a culture are adopted without understanding or respect for their significance. True empowerment through cultural exchange involves not only the sharing of cultural elements but also the acknowledgment and appreciation of their origins and meanings.

In essence, cultural exchange is a powerful catalyst for empowerment. By embracing the richness of diverse cultural expressions and fostering genuine connections, individuals and communities can create a more inclusive and harmonious world. Through understanding and collaboration, cultural exchange paves the way for a future where differences are celebrated and collective strength is cultivated.

Fostering Inclusion

Creating an inclusive setting is not only a moral issue but also a practical strategy that increases productivity, creativity, and well-being in any organization or society. Inclusion is about establishing the sense of belonging where everyone feels valued and respected regardless of background, ability, or opinion.

In the spirit of "Empower, Don't Overpower," inclusion is key to empowering people and groups to contribute their best to the organization. It is about acknowledging and appreciating diversity in all its dimensions beyond the self-evident dimensions of race, gender, or age to include less apparent dimensions such as thought diversity, education, and experience as well.

To really foster inclusion, it is first necessary to know and understand the barriers to complete participation of individuals. They can be systemic, i.e., policies or practices that inadvertently exclude certain people, or cultural, i.e., biases and stereotypes embedded in behavior and decision-making. To combat these barriers, one must take an active approach, starting with awareness and education. It is possible to train people on unconscious bias, cultural competence, and empathy, making them aware of their own biases and at least trying to view the world from others' perspectives.

Communication is the core of inclusion building. Communication that is open and honest makes people feel free to express their ideas and experiences without fear of judgment or punishment. Providing space for this kind of communication in the form of regular meetings, forums, or social events is the core of trust and cohesion building among people in a community. Lastly, the provision of communication to everyone regardless of their language or ability is the basis of inclusive practice.

Leadership commitment is also a key element in building inclusion. Leaders set the tone for the organization or the community as a whole. Leaders practice inclusive behavior when they look for diverse input proactively and appreciate the inputs of all members. Leaders set the values of inclusion when they practice such behavior and get others to do so as well. Leaders must also commit to holding themselves and others accountable for building an inclusive environment, for example, in the speedy and effective resolution of acts of discrimination or exclusion.

Practices and policies must also be dedicated to inclusion and may include the allocation of flexible work arrangements to meet different needs, updating hiring and recruitment practices to ensure diversity, and developing clear respective behavior policies. Measuring and evaluating the effectiveness of inclusion efforts can also yield useful information and help to make improvements over time.

Building inclusion is an ongoing process that requires dedication and persistence from everyone involved. It is about building spaces where people can be themselves and where their diversity is not only tolerated but celebrated. By prioritizing inclusion, organizations and communities can unlock the potential of their members and gain higher innovation, resilience, and success. In "Empower, Don't Overpower," the emphasis on inclusion is rooted in the belief that empowering others leads to bigger, more cohesive communities and organizations where everyone can thrive. thrive.

EMPOWERMENT AND POLICY

"Policy becomes powerful when it uplifts every voice and dismantles invisible barriers."

— Dr. Balvinder S. Banga

Chapter - 11

Civic Empowerment & Systemic Influence

Creating Inclusive Policies

Developing policies that facilitate inclusiveness in organizations is the basic process of making a place where everyone is valued and respected. Inclusiveness is not a fad but a required method of bringing diverse voices to the table and being represented. Developing such policies requires a close understanding of the distinct needs and ideas of all members of the organization.

The initial step in developing inclusive policies is to acknowledge the varied nature of the workforce. This includes the acknowledgment of race, gender, age, ability, and other aspects of identity differences that create diversity in the organizational setting. Policies must be developed in a manner that it positively addresses the differences so that no group feels marginalized or excluded.

One such effective method is by holding open forums with employees. Gathering inputs from different groups can yield useful information regarding the issues they are experiencing and improvements they would want to experience. This process of participation does not only assist in the identification of particular issues but also employee empowerment by engaging them in the policy-making process. There must be safe areas where employees are free to share their first-hand experiences and inputs without fear of retaliation.

The second and no less critical is to incorporate inclusivity into the organizational culture. Policies should not be isolated but be integrated into a larger strategy by training programs, awareness campaigns, and management support. Training programs will ensure employees become aware of unconscious biases and are equipped with the knowledge to interact respectfully and inclusively with others. Awareness campaigns will ensure employees understand the benefits of inclusivity, which are higher creativity, better problem-solving, and higher employee satisfaction.

Leadership is central to the successful adoption of inclusive policies. The leaders should set the example and actively encourage the firm's values. They should be educated on how to identify and overcome bias, build diverse teams, and provide equal opportunity to all in the organization. Leadership buy-in is necessary in placing inclusivity in the organization's culture to make it an integral part of the organization's DNA and not a fringe program.

Another critical aspect is testing inclusive policies. Organizations need to have monitoring processes to measure the effectiveness of their policies and make adjustments as necessary. This is done through monitoring diversity metrics, conducting employee surveys, and monitoring representation of diverse groups within the management. Regular monitoring ensures policies are effective and relevant in maintaining inclusivity.

In addition, the creation of inclusive policies has to be a dynamic and adaptive process. As society's norms and values evolve, so must policies governing workplace behavior. Firms have to be open and responsive to change and to modifying their policies to fit fresh ideas about inclusivity and diversity.

Fundamentally, the creation of inclusive policies is not about compliance, but rather about creating a setting where everyone feels included and empowered within the organization. In prioritizing inclusivity in policy-making, organizations are in a position to unlock the full potential of their diverse workforce, which leads to a more innovative, productive, and harmonious workplace. Through crafting inclusive policies through deliberate and meticulous consideration, organizations are able to effectively empower their workers, creating a culture of respect and equality for all.

Advocacy and Change

In the areas of personal and social empowerment, advocacy efforts cannot be overemphasized. Advocacy is the connecting link between the identification of the need for change and the actual implementation of the change in a practical manner. Advocacy is a very effective tool that enables individuals and communities to articulate their needs, break the norm, and initiate system change.

Essentially, advocacy is a question of representing those who otherwise would possess no voice or would be disregarded. It is founded on the assumption that all human beings, regardless of what their circumstances are, ought to be heard and have some influence in the decisions that shape their lives. Advocacy is an active process of education, communication, and action. It requires a firm understanding of the issues involved, and the ability to articulate these issues persuasively to those in authority.

One of advocacy's underlying assumptions is that advocacy is empowerment, and not control. Advocates ally with individuals and communities, giving them tools and assistance they need to advocate for themselves. This practice creates ownership and leadership because individuals are encouraged to become active participants in their own destiny. Advocacy empowerment is not about mandating solutions but about establishing spaces where many can be included in the discussion.

Change, via advocacy, is typically incremental. It requires hard work and time, planning. Advocates must navigate complex systems and must overcome opposition from those who benefit from the status quo. But even incremental change can be profoundly transformative. Each step forward can be a catalyst to more action, with a ripple effect that ultimately equates to broader society change.

There are several important steps involved in the advocacy process. The process begins with the identification of issues to be addressed and their root causes. This usually entails research and consultation with experts as well as people directly affected by the issues. Second, advocates aim to create awareness and mobilize public support. This can entail mounting campaigns, media work, or lobbying governments.

Successful advocacy also involves the formation of coalitions and alliances. Through the coming together of similar people and organizations, the advocate is able to have more leverage and enhance their chance of success. The coalitions can provide higher bases of support and resources and greater diversity of viewpoints that enrich the advocacy cause.

Lastly, advocacy is attempting to initiate change that is equitable and sustainable. Advocacy is about creating contexts in which equity and justice are a consideration, in which all have an opportunity to be their best. Advocacy is a manifestation of the power of collective action and a belief that change is possible when people unite with a shared vision.

Empowerment, when coupled with successful advocacy, is a driver of revolutionary change. Empowerment overturns oppressive systems and builds new paradigms that establish human dignity and respect as paramount. As we delve further into the subject of empowerment throughout this book, the position of advocacy continues to be a mainstay in working towards a more just and equitable world.

Considering the use of inclusive policies, it is helpful to rely on the real impact of listening and advocacy in the world.

Policy Implementation

Effective policy implementation is crucial in ensuring that empowerment strategies are successfully executed and yield the desired outcomes. The process involves translating policy objectives into actionable steps that foster an environment where empowerment can flourish without overwhelming or undermining individuals.

A key aspect of successful policy implementation is clarity. Policies must be clearly articulated and communicated to all stakeholders involved. This ensures that everyone understands their roles, responsibilities, and the goals of the policy. Clear communication helps to align the efforts of various departments and individuals, minimizing confusion and preventing overlapping efforts that could lead to inefficiencies.

Moreover, adequate resources must be allocated to support the implementation process. This includes financial resources, human capital, and technological tools that facilitate the execution of empowerment strategies. Without sufficient resources, even the most well-intentioned policies may falter. Ensuring that resources are appropriately distributed allows for a smoother implementation process and increases the likelihood of achieving policy objectives.

Another critical component is the establishment of a robust monitoring and evaluation framework. This framework should be designed to track the progress of policy implementation and assess its impact. By continuously monitoring outcomes, organizations can identify potential obstacles and adjust their strategies accordingly. Evaluation provides valuable insights into what works and what doesn't, enabling policymakers to refine their approaches and optimize results.

Stakeholder engagement is also vital in the policy implementation process. Engaging with those who are affected by the policies, including employees, community members, and other relevant parties, helps to build support and foster a sense of ownership. When stakeholders feel involved and heard, they are more likely to embrace the changes and contribute positively to the policy's success. Engagement also provides opportunities for feedback, which can be invaluable in refining policy measures to better meet the needs of those it aims to empower.

Leadership plays a pivotal role in guiding policy implementation. Leaders must champion the empowerment initiatives, demonstrating commitment and setting an example for others to follow. Strong leadership helps to maintain momentum and motivate stakeholders to remain focused on the goals. Leaders also have the responsibility to address any resistance to change, providing support and reassurance to those who may be hesitant about the new policies.

Flexibility is another important consideration. The implementation process should be adaptable to changing circumstances and emerging challenges. Policies that are too rigid may fail to accommodate unforeseen developments, hindering progress and potentially leading to policy failure. Flexibility allows organizations to remain responsive and innovative, making necessary adjustments to stay on track towards empowerment goals.

In essence, successful policy implementation requires a strategic and coordinated effort that considers clarity, resource allocation, monitoring, stakeholder engagement, leadership, and flexibility. By focusing on these elements, organizations can create a conducive environment for empowerment, ensuring that policies not only set the stage for positive change but also translate into tangible and sustainable outcomes. Through effective implementation, empowerment becomes a shared journey where individuals are supported to reach their full potential without the constraints of overpowering directives.

Measuring Impact

It takes a comprehensive approach to measuring impact in order to understand the effect of empowerment in an organization. Applying empowerment strategies alone is not enough, organizations must track their outcomes to confirm that they are receiving what they anticipate. This is a qualitative and quantitative analysis process that can be used to shape future decisions and growth.

One way of measuring the effect of empowerment can be through employee performance measures. This can come in the way of productivity, quality, and innovation levels. Pre- and post-measurement on comparison after implementing empowerment measures, organizations can see the impact of their efforts. Improved productivity and innovation are generally positive indicators, as empowered employees take the initiative themselves and bring innovative inputs to their jobs.

Employee satisfaction surveys are also a significant measure of impact. Surveys let you know how employees feel about their job and the company in general. Job satisfaction is greatest when employees feel empowered, as they are valued and motivated when they feel accountable and in charge. Surveys can be utilized to track some aspects of empowerment, such as decision-making authority, resources available, and recognition for effort.

Customer feedback is also a useful indicator of the impact of empowerment. Improved service by empowered staff can lead to customer satisfaction and loyalty. Customer feedback and satisfaction metrics can lead organizations to decide if their empowerment programs are having a positive impact on their customers. Customer feedback may also highlight areas for improvement that can be utilized to further evolve empowerment practice.

Organizations must also consider the impact of empowerment on working together and collaboration. Empowered employees are more inclined to engage in healthy collaboration, information sharing, and coordination of activities. Observations of team interactions and evaluation of team members can tell one if empowerment is developing a culture of teamwork. This can be measured by team performance and team member feedback.

Quantitative data must be accompanied by qualitative data to better comprehend the effects of empowerment. Focus groups and interviews can yield more detailed insight into what the employees think and feel. The interviews can disclose vast information about the empowerment issues and why empowerment is effective.

Organizations must have well-defined targets and objectives for empowerment programs. The targets must be well-defined in terms of the organization's overall objectives and reviewed from time to time to determine whether they are still valid. Having well-defined, measurable targets will enable organizations to assess the effectiveness of their empowerment programs better.

Example:

A logistics company implemented an empowerment initiative that allowed warehouse staff to suggest process improvements and make certain operational decisions independently. Within three months, package processing time improved by 18%, and error rates dropped by 12%. Employee satisfaction surveys revealed a 25% increase in engagement, particularly in areas related to feeling valued and heard. Customer feedback also improved, reflecting higher satisfaction with service quality. Supervisors observed enhanced team collaboration as employees initiated daily huddles on their own. Based on these findings, the company expanded the program and made it part of their long-term strategy. This case demonstrates how measuring both qualitative and quantitative outcomes can help validate and refine empowerment efforts.

Lastly, it is an ongoing process of measurement of empowerment that requires commitment and adaptability. Organizations must be willing to alter their approach depending on what they are measuring and open to feedback from employees at all levels. Through ongoing measurement and adjustment of their processes, organizations can cultivate an empowerment culture that not only enhances the performance of the individual but also organizational performance. This focus on measurement and adjustment makes empowerment not a fad but a functional and working part of the organization's strategy.

"Empathy emerges as a cornerstone of leadership during turbulent times."

— Dr. Balvinder S. Banga

Chapter - 12

Empowerment in Crisis Management

Leading Through Uncertainty

In the modern age of uncertainty where the only certainty is uncertainty, good leadership demands a high-level approach. The old paradigms that in the past offered a model for strategy and decision-making are now overshadowed by rapid technological advancements, worldwide crises, and shifting expectations of society. Leaders are required to navigate through this uncertainty by showing ***resilience, flexibility, and foresight.*** The art of leading in uncertainty is in being able to remain grounded while being agile enough to change direction as circumstances shift. This dualism demands an in-depth understanding of one's vision and values so that decisions are always in the direction of the organization's core purpose. By looking at transparency and openness, leaders can create a culture of trust where members feel safe when the destination is unknown. Perhaps the most powerful resource a leader can leverage is the creation of a culture of learning in an organization. Fostering continuous learning and development gives team members the capability to respond to the unforeseen challenges. The focus on learning should be complemented by leaders themselves, being open to new ideas and suggestions and new ways of thinking. During uncertainty, leaders need to be scenario planning masters. The process is as much about developing flexible plans to fight a string of probable futures as it is about imagining a string of probable futures. Through scenario analysis, leaders can reduce the risk and capture opportunities that will necessarily arrive unexpectedly. Forethought can effectively eliminate the fear of uncertainty that would otherwise be present, resulting in a sense of control in the face of uncertainty. **Empathy is the leadership strategy in the midst of uncertainty**. Knowledge of the psychological and emotional effects of uncertainty on team members enables leaders to offer the support and encouragement required. **By creating a sense of belongingness, where each voice is heard and each idea valued, leaders are well-positioned to unlock the collective genius of their teams, leading to innovation and problem-solving**.

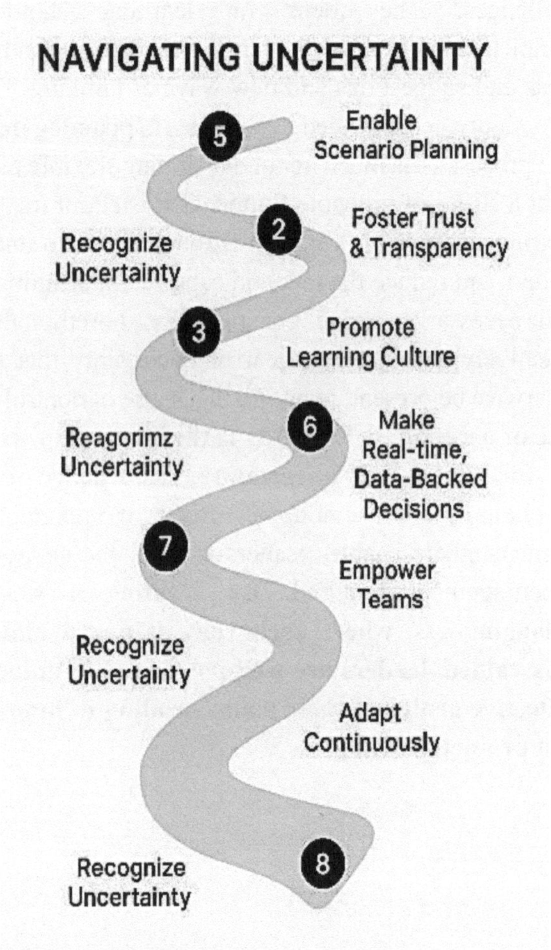

In addition, decision-making amidst uncertainty requires greater agility. Leaders must be ready to make reality-based decisions in real-time, without paralyzing themselves with analysis. This entails a reliance on instincts seasoned by experience and data and vulnerability to feedback and course correction. The capacity to remain decisive yet humble in the face of changing circumstances is the hallmark of good leadership. The use of technology cannot be overlooked in navigating uncertainty. Utilizing digital platforms and data analysis has the potential to offer timely information to help the leader make reality-based decisions based on facts. By using technology, leaders can de-bureaucratize and enable communication, leading to a more connected and responsive organization. A culture of resilience and agility that goes beyond having all the answers is necessary for leadership during uncertainty. The goal is to empower individuals in the organization to take ownership of their role and make meaningful contributions towards the collective goals. Leaders can use uncertainty as a platform for innovation and growth, leading their organizations into a future of promise and possibility by living these values. The journey through uncertainty is a testament to the strength and potential of empowered leadership.

Psychological First Aid

In periods of crisis, the human mind is likely to face issues that appear impossible to resolve. **Psychological First Aid** (PFA) assists in the treatment of short-term needs of crisis individuals, allowing them to recover a sense of control and safety. Unlike conventional therapeutic treatment, PFA is more focused on short-term needs and less interested in long-term mental health interventions. PFA is an empathic evidence-based intervention that is focused on alleviating immediate distress as well as enhancing adaptive functioning. **The essence of PFA is active listening**. This entails offering uninterrupted attention to the individual, labeling emotion, and validating experience without judgment. Such empathic contact can travel a long way in alleviating feelings of isolation and helplessness and offering a sense of belongingness and understanding. The provider has to be calm in demeanor, thereby helping to reassure the concerned individual, making the environment recovery-friendly. The second vital aspect of PFA is the offer of practical support. This entails helping individuals to list out their short-term needs, for example, food, shelter, or medical care, and helping them to access these interventions. By tending to these tangible issues, PFA stabilizes the environment, allowing individuals to focus on their emotional and psychological recovery. PFA also focuses significantly on empowering people. This involves helping them to access their strengths and resilience, reminding them of coping strategies that were effective in the past. Empowerment is focused on giving people a sense of agency, such that they feel empowered to take small, realistic steps to recovery.

This approach not only allows crisis management on the spot but also lays the groundwork for long-term resilience. **Communication is a second mainstay of PFA**. Providing clear, concise information about the situation and available resources can decrease anxiety and confusion. Communication must be tailored to the level of understanding of the individual so that they feel informed and included in decision-making. Honesty and transparency are imperative because they build trust and credibility between the provider and the individual. The importance of cultural sensitivity cannot be overemphasized in the provision of PFA. Attentiveness and respect for cultural differences are fundamental to good support. This means knowledge of cultural norms, values, and communication patterns and awareness of any potential biases that may affect the interaction. Culturally sensitive provision ensures support is useful and respectful, thus more effective. It is crucial for providers of PFA to take care of themselves. It's important for providers to be aware of their own limitations and seek help when necessary when providing emotional support to those in distress. By maintaining ongoing self-care, they can maintain their capacity to provide effective support to others. Psychological First Aid is a valuable tool in crisis response, providing immediate intervention and establishing resilience. Through active listening, practical care, empowerment, communication, cultural sensitivity, and self-care, PFA provides a holistic process for addressing the immediate psychological needs of distressed individuals. ***It is the epitome of "Empower, Don't Overpower," with emphasis on support, understanding, and teamwork in recovery.***

Resilience in Teams

In today's fast-paced and rapidly changing work environment, the ability to withstand and bounce back from adversity is critical to long-term success. **Resilience, or the ability to bounce back from adversity, is not only an individual quality but an absolute team quality as well.** Resilient teams can withstand the challenges of their work, maintain productivity, and build a positive culture that fosters growth and innovation. **Communication is the key to a resilient team.** Open lines of communication allow team members to voice concerns, share ideas, and collaborate to find solutions. Not only does this build trust among members, but it also fosters a culture of respect and trust. When team members are heard and understood, they will be more apt to contribute positively and rally around one another during challenging times. Another critical component of team resilience is adaptability. In a world of constant change, teams must be able to adapt in their problem-solving function. This means a culture of embracing new ideas and solutions, as well as the capability to change strategies when circumstances require it. Encouraging a culture of continuous learning and development allows teams to be responsive and adaptable to changing circumstances.

Figure: The Resilient Team Wheel-Eight core components of a resilient, high-performing team

Leadership also plays a key role in developing resilience within teams. Good leaders lead and shepherd the team members through uncertainty and adversity. Leaders themselves are resilient in action, demonstrating to their team members how to remain calm in the midst of chaos and see failure as a chance to learn. By developing a culture in which team members can afford to take initiative and make decisions, leaders become able to develop ownership and accountability that makes the team as a whole more resilient. A resilient team is also a diverse and inclusive team. Diverse teams have a wealth of ideas and experience, which can be translated into more innovative solutions and more problem-solving ability. By developing an inclusive culture in which every team member feels respected and valued, teams can leverage their strengths as a whole to weather adversity and get the job done. A support system within the team is also key in developing resilience. Team members must feel free to call for help when they need it and offer support to others. This esprit de corps prevents any team member from feeling alone in adversity, and it reinforces the fact that the team is a whole greater than the sum of its parts. Celebrating small wins, no matter how small, and recognizing the hard work and determination of team members can also help further enhance morale and reinforce positive team culture. Resilience in teams is finally maintained by ensuring a healthy work-life balance. By assisting team members in prioritizing their own well-being and taking time to rest and recover, burnout is avoided, and they are able to continue contributing in a meaningful way. Flexible work arrangements and mental health assistance can do wonders for a resilient team culture. By focusing on these two areas, teams can become resilient enough to thrive in the midst of challenge. Resilience is a process, one that requires effort and persistence from every team member. But the reward of a **resilient team improved collaboration, improved problem-solving capabilities, and an improved work climate are well within grasp**.

Restoring Confidence and Morale

In the dynamic world of leadership, one of the most important challenges is to restore and sustain confidence and morale among team members. This assignment becomes very important when the team experiences setbacks, either due to external circumstances or internal dynamics. Leaders need to come up with strategies that not only solve immediate issues but also create a resilient and empowered workforce capable of meeting future challenges. One of the key steps toward restoring confidence and morale is creating an open communication environment. Encouraging team members to voice their concerns, fears, and ideas without fear of reprisal is essential. Leaders should listen actively and appreciate these inputs, showing empathy and understanding. This method not only validates the feelings of team members but also creates trust, a foundation of a united and motivated team. Another great tool is having well-defined and achievable goals. When teams experience failure, the overall goals are too much to accomplish. Breaking them into smaller, achievable goals can build confidence. Celebrating small victories along the way reinforces a sense of success and movement, motivating team members to work toward bigger goals. Leaders also need to use the tool of empowering team members by assigning them tasks to complete and learning opportunities to build talent. Empowerment introduces a sense of responsibility and ownership, which can greatly increase morale. When team members feel valued and trusted, their confidence in their skills and their worth to the success of the team is heightened. Appreciation and recognition are potent tools in rebuilding morale. Public acknowledgment of individual and team effort can be a huge motivational boost. Appreciation needs to be specific and sincere, with recognition of the individual contribution of each team member. This not only increases individual confidence but also creates a culture of optimism and respect. Leaders must also model optimism and resilience lastly. What they do dictates the tone of the team, and the exhibition of a positive attitude in the face of adversity can be contagious. By being **solution-focused instead of problem-focused**, leaders can instill the same in their teams. Feedback loops are also needed in the process. Positive feedback aids team members to understand areas for improvement while reinforcing strengths. Bi-weekly feedback sessions should be given in an uplifting tone, focusing on growth and development instead of criticism. Providing opportunities for team bonding can also bolster morale. Collaborative events and camaraderie events establish a network of support where team members are committed and aligned. Whether for team-building exercises, social gatherings, collaborative ventures, or other activities, these events establish interdependence and belongingness. Finally, **leaders should be transparent about failure and setbacks**. Transparency about the situation and action to correct the situation can remove ambiguity and build confidence in the team members. Transparency establishes a culture of trust and accountability, the key ingredients in building confidence and morale. Through the execution of these processes, leaders can rebuild confidence and morale among their teams. Not only does this enhance the performance of the group in the short term, but it also lays the ground for a solid, empowered workforce that can withstand future storms with confidence and resilience.

"Financial literacy transforms survival into security, and ambition into achievement. It's not just about money—it's about the power to live with purpose and freedom."

— Dr. Balvinder S. Banga

Chapter - 13

Empowerment through Financial Literacy

Why Money Knowledge Equals Power

Understanding money is not just about managing your finances, but you have to know how to utilize your money as a tool to change your future and the world you live in. When you understand how to utilize money as a good tool, it can change your life. Knowing and dealing with money is not natural; it's a feeling of having power that doesn't have anything to do with money. The first reason that money knowledge makes you powerful is that it helps you make good choices without someone else telling you what you have to do. By understanding about money and making choices that are in harmony with their values and objectives, people are in a position to deal with the complexity of both their own and the world's economies. This independence helps people feel in charge of their lives, which makes them less reliant on outside forces and more able to make their own choices. Financial literacy helps people have the tools that they need to plan for and respond to changes in the economy. People are able to place themselves strategically, protect their assets, and maximize their opportunities for growth by learning about trends in the marketplace, interest rates, and investing. This proactive attitude not only protects wealth but also uncovers new ways of growing it, which gives a person more power and choices in society.

To level the playing field, individuals must learn about money. Learning about money could be a huge way to level the playing field in a world where economic inequality is always an issue. Individuals can create a sound financial future by learning how to budget, save, and invest. This will result in a more equitable distribution of opportunities. Understanding about money also empowers individuals to speak out for themselves and other individuals. Individuals who understand about money can participate in informed discussions about policy and practice that impact their communities. This type of campaigning can result in changes in the system that benefit both individuals and large numbers of individuals. Intelligent citizens can assist in making legislation better, encourage fair business practices, and hold institutions to account, all of which can contribute to society's advancement. Don't forget how good it is for your brain to understand about money. Being financially astute may assist you in coping with the strain and anxiety that arise from not knowing what is going to happen to the economy. Individuals feel secure and comfortable when they understand about how much money they have and have a plan for it. This clarity allows them to concentrate on other areas of their lives, which is good for their health and well-being. Understanding about money may also assist you to develop new ideas and start your own business.

Individuals may start and operate businesses more readily when they understand how money operates. This results in economic growth and job creation. The spirit of entrepreneurship can make people succeed on their own terms and contribute to the economy, and that is good for everyone. Learning about money can empower you even more. People are endowed with the power they need to fulfill their dreams and leave a mark. We can make power not in the hands of a few people but in the hands of those who wish to use it for the greater good by making money accessible and understandable to everyone. Learning about money is not just about personal success; it can make communities better and help make the world a better place.

To understand how financial knowledge can quietly transform lives, consider the story of Rina—a woman who turned a ledger into her ladder.

📘 Rina's Ledger: A Story of Quiet Empowerment

In a narrow lane of a bustling town in Punjab, **Rina**, a young mother of two, ran a small tailoring shop from her home. Her talent with a needle was unmatched, but her finances were always slipping through her fingers. Each month, she worked hard—but never knew where her money went.

One evening, during a local community meeting, Rina hesitantly attended a session on **basic financial literacy**. The concept of budgeting and saving was foreign to her—but something clicked. That night, she opened an old school notebook and created her first budget, titled: *"Rina's Ledger"*.

She began tracking every rupee. She set aside ₹50 a week, no matter what. She stopped impulse purchases. Within six months, she had saved enough to buy a better sewing machine. A year later, she expanded into children's wear. Her income doubled.

More importantly, she no longer feared money—she understood it.

When her younger daughter asked how she did it, Rina smiled and said, "I didn't earn more. I learned more."

Rina now teaches local women how to budget, save, and invest. Her story isn't one of sudden wealth—but of **steady empowerment**, built one thoughtful decision at a time.

Rina's story is a powerful example of how even simple financial literacy principles—budgeting, saving, and tracking expenses—can change the course of a person's life. Let's now explore how to build that same foundation.

Foundations First- Budgeting, Saving & Responsible Spending Establishing a solid financial foundation is like laying the groundwork for a sturdy house. The key components-**budgeting, saving, and responsible spending** serve as the essential pillars that uphold financial stability and growth. Each element plays a distinct role, yet they are interconnected, creating a harmonious balance that fosters financial well-being. Budgeting is the cornerstone of this foundation. It involves creating a plan that outlines income and expenses, enabling individuals to allocate resources effectively. A well-crafted budget provides clarity and control, allowing for informed financial decisions. It is not merely a tool for tracking expenses but a proactive strategy that empowers individuals to prioritize their financial goals. By understanding where money comes from and where it goes, one can identify areas where adjustments are needed, thus preventing unnecessary expenditure and promoting savings. Saving is the next crucial element, acting as a safety net for unforeseen circumstances and a catalyst for future aspirations. Establishing a habit of saving requires discipline and commitment. It begins with setting realistic goals, whether it be an emergency fund, a down payment on a home, or retirement savings. The act of saving cultivates a sense of security and independence, reducing reliance on credit and debt. Automated savings plans can facilitate this process by ensuring a portion of income is consistently set aside, thereby eliminating the temptation to spend impulsively. Responsible spending is the third pillar, encompassing the mindful and intentional use of money. It is about making choices that align with one's values and long-term objectives. Responsible spending involves distinguishing between needs and wants, a skill that requires ongoing reflection and self- awareness. It encourages individuals to evaluate their spending habits and make conscious decisions that contribute to their overall financial health. By prioritizing expenditures that add genuine value to their lives, individuals can avoid the pitfalls of consumerism and debt. Together, these foundational elements create a robust financial framework that supports both short-term stability and long-term prosperity. They encourage a shift from reactive to proactive financial management, empowering individuals to take control of their economic destiny. This foundation is not static; it evolves alongside changing circumstances and goals. Regular review and adjustment are essential to ensure continued alignment with personal aspirations and financial realities. Building and maintaining this foundation requires education and practice. **Financial literacy plays a pivotal role in understanding the principles and tools necessary for effective budgeting, saving, and spending**. Access to resources, whether through workshops, online courses, or financial advisors, can enhance one's ability to make informed decisions. Moreover, cultivating a supportive environment, where open discussions about finances are encouraged, can further reinforce these practices, making them a natural part of daily life. In the quest for financial empowerment, the principles of budgeting, saving, and responsible spending serve as guiding lights. They provide the framework within which individuals can navigate the complexities of modern finance, laying the groundwork for a future that is not only secure but fulfilling. **By embracing these foundational elements, individuals can transform their financial landscape, fostering resilience and enabling them to thrive in an ever-changing world**.

Digital Finance- Unlocking Access, Managing Risks

In the rapidly evolving landscape of modern economics, digital finance has emerged as a pivotal force capable of reshaping financial accessibility and risk management. As digital platforms proliferate, they democratize financial services, extending them beyond traditional boundaries and into the hands of the underserved. This expansion offers unprecedented opportunities for individuals and businesses alike, while simultaneously introducing new challenges in risk management. Digital finance encompasses a myriad of services, including mobile banking, digital wallets, peer-to-peer lending, and cryptocurrencies, each contributing to a more inclusive financial ecosystem. Mobile banking, for instance, enables consumers in remote areas to access banking services without the need for physical branches. This has been transformative in regions where traditional banking infrastructure is limited, providing a critical lifeline for financial inclusion. Digital wallets further enhance accessibility by allowing users to store and manage funds electronically. They offer a convenient and secure alternative to cash, facilitating transactions ranging from everyday purchases to international remittances. The ease of use and widespread adoption of these platforms have empowered individuals who previously struggled with the complexities of traditional banking systems. Peer-to-peer lending platforms have revolutionized access to credit by connecting borrowers directly with lenders. This model bypasses conventional financial institutions, reducing costs and expanding the pool of available credit. For small businesses and entrepreneurs, this can mean the difference between stagnation and growth, enabling them to secure funding that might otherwise be inaccessible. Cryptocurrencies, while still in their nascent stages, present a unique opportunity to redefine financial transactions. By offering decentralized and borderless money transfer capabilities, cryptocurrencies can potentially reduce transaction costs and enhance financial inclusivity on a global scale. However, their volatility and regulatory uncertainties necessitate careful consideration and management. While the benefits of digital finance are substantial, they are not without risks. The digital nature of these services introduces vulnerabilities, including cybersecurity threats and fraud. As financial transactions move online, protecting sensitive data becomes paramount. Financial institutions and technology providers must invest in robust security measures to safeguard user information and maintain trust. Moreover, the rapid pace of innovation in digital finance can outstrip regulatory frameworks, leading to gaps in oversight. Regulators are tasked with the challenge of balancing innovation with consumer protection, ensuring that new financial products do not exploit or harm users. Effective regulation requires a nuanced understanding of technology and collaboration between stakeholders to create frameworks that evolve in tandem with technological advancements. Financial literacy is also a crucial component in managing risks associated with digital finance. As access to financial services increases, so too does the need for education on the responsible use of these tools. Empowering individuals with the knowledge to navigate digital finance safely and effectively can mitigate risks and enhance the benefits of financial inclusion. In this dynamic environment, digital finance stands as a double-edged sword. It holds the promise of unlocking access to financial services for millions, driving economic empowerment and growth.

However, it also demands vigilant management of the inherent risks to ensure that the power of digital finance is harnessed responsibly and equitably. As stakeholders work together to navigate this complex landscape, the potential for digital finance to transform lives becomes increasingly tangible, offering a future where financial empowerment is accessible to all.

Financial Inclusion- Reaching Women, Youth & Marginalized Voices

In In a universe where money too frequently decides who gets to participate in opportunity, economic empowerment is not only a policy imperative -it's a lifeline. But millions of people -especially women, youth, and the poor are excluded from economic systems. They're not lacking in potential; they're lacking in access. Closing this gap is not only the right thing to do it's one of the best investments we can make in a more inclusive, more prosperous future.

Look at women, for example. They're nearly half of the planet, yet so many of them still face unseen barriers to money management or economic opportunity. Sometimes it's culture. Sometimes it's because they're not offered products that address their lives like flexible loans, micro-business savings accounts, or even simply a bank that they can enter. Too frequently left out of the discussion is that economically empowering women not only changes their lives it raises families, communities, and economies. The story of **Grameen Bank in Bangladesh** is proof millions of women given small loans, who then went on to create big change.

And then there's the youth. Bright, ambitious, creative yet frequently excluded from financial systems simply because they're young. No credit history. Limited income. Policies that assume they're too risky. But here's the truth, today's young people are tomorrow's entrepreneurs, educators, and leaders. Give them the tools early like financial literacy programs, zero-minimum balance accounts, or micro-loans to kick start a small idea and they'll not only learn to manage money, they'll use it to fuel innovation. In many parts of the world, mobile apps are helping them do just that.

Marginalized groups like indigenous communities, people in remote areas, or racial minorities—face an even more uphill battle. It's not just distance from the nearest bank. It's discrimination. It's being overlooked. It's not having the internet to even check a balance. But there's hope here, too. Kenya's M-Pesa brought banking to the palms of people's hands. India, too, is making remarkable strides through digital-first, grassroots-led initiatives.

Take India Post Payments Bank (IPPB), for example, which uses the post office network to bring doorstep banking to the farthest villages. Postmen and women now carry handheld devices that enable you to open an account, transfer money, or pay a bill—without having to set foot in a bank. Or take Paytm Payments Bank and Airtel Payments Bank, which turn any smartphone or even a feature phone into a banking terminal, giving the user instant access to money, anywhere. Fino Payments Bank and Spice Money go further by building hyperlocal banking networks through local agents, bringing financial services to those who've never seen a branch.

These innovations prove that **banking in hand is not just a slogan in India -it's a revolution** that gives power to rural women, migrant workers, and small traders.

But none of this happens in isolation. Governments, banks, tech innovators, and nonprofits must work together crafting policies that protect people, building products that serve all walks of life, and ensuring no one's left behind. It's also about changing the conversation. Inclusion isn't charity it's smart economics. When we expand access, we expand what's possible for everyone.

Of course, real empowerment goes beyond numbers. It's not just about how many accounts are opened it's about how many lives are truly changed. That's why financial inclusion must be intentional, intersectional, and ongoing. We must recognize how barriers overlap how being a young woman in a rural area, for instance, brings a unique set of challenges. And we must design solutions that reflect those realities.

Financial empowerment isn't just about opening doors it's about walking with people through them. It's about making sure women can invest in their dreams, youth can take bold first steps, and every person regardless of where they come from can build a future they believe in. Because when that happens, we're not just fixing systems we're changing lives. And that, ultimately, is how real progress begins.

From Earning to Empowering: Building Sustainable Financial Futures

The transition from merely earning an income to empowering oneself financially requires a fundamental shift in mindset and approach. It involves moving beyond the traditional notions of income generation to developing sustainable financial strategies that provide long-term security and growth opportunities. At the core of this transformation lies the need for financial literacy, strategic planning, and an understanding of the broader economic forces at play. Financial literacy is the cornerstone of empowerment. Understanding basic financial concepts such as budgeting, saving, investing, and managing debt is crucial. These skills enable individuals to make informed decisions that align with their long-term goals. For instance, budgeting is not just about tracking expenses; it's about prioritizing spending to ensure that financial resources are allocated effectively to support both immediate needs and future ambitions. **Investing is another critical component in the journey towards financial empowerment**. It is not solely about building wealth but also about creating opportunities for passive income, which can provide financial stability and freedom. The key is to diversify investments across different asset classes, such as stocks, bonds, real estate, and mutual funds, which can mitigate risks and maximize returns. Understanding the market trends and economic indicators can further enhance investment strategies, allowing individuals to capitalize on opportunities and safeguard against potential downturns. Debt management is equally essential in building a sustainable financial future. While some debt can be beneficial, such as mortgages or student loans that contribute to asset building and personal growth, high-interest consumer debt can be detrimental. Developing a plan to minimize and eliminate unnecessary debt is crucial. This involves negotiating better terms, consolidating loans, and making regular payments to reduce the principal amount quickly. Another vital aspect of financial empowerment is cultivating a mindset of resilience and adaptability. The economic landscape is continually evolving, and the ability to adapt to changes is crucial for long-term financial success. This involves staying informed about economic policies, market shifts, and emerging trends that could impact personal finances. By remaining flexible and open to new opportunities, individuals can navigate challenges and seize new prospects that align with their financial goals. Moreover, empowering oneself financially also means understanding the social and environmental impacts of financial decisions. Sustainable investing, for example, focuses on supporting companies and projects that prioritize environmental, social, and governance (ESG) criteria. This approach not only contributes to personal financial growth but also promotes positive societal change, aligning personal values with financial practices. Ultimately, building a sustainable financial future is about more than just accumulating wealth. It is about creating a foundation that supports personal growth, security, and the ability to contribute positively to the community and environment.

📘 Case Story: "My Journey into Conscious Investing"

After years of careful and prudent saving, I began to look at my options, I paused to ask a deeper question ***Where is my money going, and what is it building for the future?*** I wasn't seeking only return but I wanted my investments to be values-driven.

That is when I learned about sustainable investing that invests in businesses that care for the planet, are socially just, and are ethically accountable. I invested in an ESG fund that invested in renewable energy ventures, women-owned businesses, and ethically responsible businesses that are good for everyone.

Over time, I saw my investments grow not just financially, but emotionally. I discovered that one of the companies I had invested in was installing solar panels on rural schools. Another was making quality, accessible healthcare available to more people. To learn this made me proud. My money wasn't just sitting in a fund somewhere it was doing something.

This moment taught me that wealth has nothing to do with money. It has to do with purpose. I learned that I wasn't investing, I was creating the life I want to live, one conscious decision at a time.

By prioritizing education, strategic planning, and responsible decision-making, individuals can transform their financial lives from mere earning to true empowerment, paving the way for a future that is both prosperous and sustainable.

THE FUTURE OF EMPOWERMENT

Dr. Balvinder S Banga

"The empowered future belongs to those who adapt with empathy, innovate with purpose, and lead with courage."

— Dr. Balvinder S. Banga

Chapter - 14
The Future of Empowerment

Emerging Trends

In today's fast-changing world, it is essential to know and learn from emerging trends for individuals and organizations who want to succeed. Such trends are not passing fads but meaningful movements that influence the way we live, work, and interact with one another. Learning about such trends in empowerment can be useful lessons on how to build spaces where individuals can be stimulated to develop without being eclipsed by powerful individuals or institutions.

The biggest trend is increasing emphasis on digital connectivity. As technology has developed, the world is more connected than ever before. The digital revolution has opened up new spaces for human communication, collaboration, and innovation. It has facilitated human beings to access experts, exchange information, and share with people anywhere on the planet, without being limited by the confines of the past, to usher in a more inclusive form of empowerment. Organizations and leaders who implement these digital technologies successfully can create platforms empowering voices and enabling creativity.

Decentralization of decision-making is another significant trend. Under the traditional hierarchical models, decisions were made by the few at the top with little consultation of the stakeholders in the base. There is, however, growing recognition of the diversity and empowerment benefits of involving more stakeholders in decision-making. This trend is observed across various fields, from business organizations embracing flatter organizations to governments embracing participatory forms of government. With power being decentralized, greater ownership and accountability are transferred to individuals, and this leads to more innovative solutions and contentment.

The emergence of the gig economy is also a new trend with significant implications for empowerment. With more people needing flexible work and control over their vocation, the conventional employer-employee relationship is being rewritten. The change has produced a workforce where the individuals can leverage their abilities and talents on their own terms, usually leading to increased job satisfaction and life-work integration. But the trend also has its setbacks, such as the security and benefits, where new methods need to be created to ensure empowerment not at the cost of security.

Social responsibility and sustainability are becoming a core part of empowerment narratives. With growing environmental and social consciousness, there is mounting pressure on organizations and individuals to become responsible. The trend is influencing changes in consumer behavior and recasting the business model. Empowering people to become able to make ethical choices and organizations to become sustainable is the essence of this new reality.

Similarly, mental well-being emphasis is also being integrated into empowerment. As a statement of the importance of emotional and mental wellness, initiatives are being undertaken towards developing environments conducive to mental wellness. This emphasis places an emphasis on the requirement for empathetic leadership and the development of cultures in which people feel valued and heard.

These new trends are the manifestations of the ongoing evolution of empowerment in today's world. Through the examination of the convergence of such changes, individuals and institutions can craft spaces that empower and cultivate and drive good change. Embracing such trends is not an attempt at conforming to change, but at taking the lead and crafting a world where empowerment is the cornerstone of every action and initiative.

Challenges and Opportunities

In professional and individual development, control and empowerment balance is a multifaceted terrain. It is a dynamic that is frequently described as walking the thin line of letting go of control but at the same time creating the potential of others. It demands a higher level of human dynamics and the skill to create settings in which people feel assisted and independent.

One of the biggest challenges is the inherent human desire to control. Mentors and leaders driven by the desire to control outcomes to meet expectations can unwittingly stifle creativity and initiative by imposing rigid structures. This control model can produce a culture where employees feel they are being micromanaged, eventually killing creativity and lowering morale.

Add to that differences in work style and personality, and you have yet another layer of complexity to the issue. Each individual possesses a unique set of skills, level of knowledge, and point of view. Acceptance and toleration of differences are necessary to empowerment. It does require a voluntary shift, however, from single-size-fits-all to a more differentiated style that includes and takes advantage of individual strengths. It requires tolerance for alternative thinking and the flexibility to change styles of leadership to meet different team members' needs.

Another challenge is possible resistance to empowerment itself. Some people, who are used to directive environments, may resist new freedom that empowerment entails. This may be fear of mistakes or uncertainty and result in a resistance to act. This is mitigated by establishing a culture of trust and psychological safety, where people feel free to try and learn from mistakes without fear of punishment.

Despite all these challenges, there is vast potential unleashed by empowering and not overpowering. Empowerment gives a sense of ownership and accountability, leading to greater participation and motivation. If individuals feel that their effort is valued and that they are able to contribute, then they will be willing to dedicate themselves to work and perform with excellence.

Empowerment also sparks **creativity and innovation**. By providing individuals with the freedom to experiment with new ideas and approaches, organizations are able to tap massive reservoirs of potential that lie dormant. Not only does this lead to new solutions and innovation, but also to a culture of continuous learning and adaptability. In a changing world, such responsiveness is a potent competitive advantage.

Additionally, empowerment facilitates leadership development. Once individuals are empowered to lead and make decisions, they acquire essential skills such as problem-solving, communication, and strategic thinking. This not only enhances the individual but also develops a robust leadership pipeline, which ensures long-term sustainability and success for the organization.

Essentially, the balancing act of empowerment and control is a very thin line, and one that demands a reflective form of leadership and development. Understanding the pitfalls and capitalizing on the opportunities, however, enables organizations and individuals to build environments where empowerment can flourish, resulting in a more committed, innovative, and sustainable future. The solution is to build a culture of trust, diversity of thought, and development and autonomy of all parties involved.

Innovative Strategies

In a time when traditional approaches to the problem fail, new empowerment models offer another model for considering how individuals and communities can achieve their potential. At the heart of these models is the concept of building autonomy with facilitative guidance, so that empowerment is a collaborative process rather than something that is done to individuals.

Most compelling of these is technology as an enabler. Online platforms have leveled the playing field in information and access to resources, allowing people to learn, connect, and innovate in ways heretofore unimaginable. Virtual learning platforms, for example, open up opportunities for personal and professional growth regardless of place. This not only improves people's capability but also propels a culture of ongoing learning and adjustment needed in the fast-evolving world.

In addition, the emergence of social media has revolutionized the face of community activism and engagement. The platforms are great agents of social change due to the fact that they provide leverage to the voiceless otherwise. They facilitate the creation of online communities in which people are able to share views without any kind of limitation and coordinate collective action with ease. This is a great source of empowerment, especially to marginalized communities, as it provides them with the voice to challenge the status quo as well as fight for their rights.

In organizational empowerment, leadership is increasingly participative. Leadership styles that emphasize collaboration, inclusiveness, and collective decision-making are increasingly being embraced by leaders. Firms can tap a large reservoir of ideas and perspectives by developing a culture where employees are valued and listened to. This yields more creative solutions and higher employee satisfaction and retention.

Aside from that, the design thinking methodology is also being applied in most industries to empower through creativity and empathy. The process stimulates problem-solving through deep understanding of the needs and challenges of the participants. Through the active engagement of the stakeholders in the design process, the suggested solutions are bound to be sustainable and effective. Design thinking not only empowers individuals through the ability to take an active role in coming up with the solutions but also creates a culture of experimentation and curiosity.

Another innovative approach is the emphasis on peer-to-peer learning and mentoring. The creation of support groups in which individuals can share experience and information creates a feeling of community and shared understanding. Formal and informal mentoring schemes provide guidance and advice, helping individuals to overcome obstacles and understand opportunity. The relational element is central to empowerment because it combines the strengths of individual experience and the diversity of many points of view.

Lastly, there is growing recognition of the importance of mental and emotional well-being in empowerment. Mindfulness, resilience, and emotional intelligence are inculcated through training courses that equip people with the ability to handle stress and deal with it effectively. This multi-dimensional approach is cautious in the sense that empowerment is not only attained through such external achievements but also through such inner growth and fulfillment.

New forms of empowerment are shifting our mindset and behavior regarding change. Through technology, inclusive leadership, innovative problem-solving, mentorship, and a focus on well-being, we create contexts in which people and communities flourish. These approaches value empowerment as an ongoing, evolving process that creates possibilities and resiliency in the midst of ever-changing challenges.

Innovative Approaches

In a world where traditional methods often fall short, innovative approaches to empowerment offer a fresh perspective on how individuals and communities can unlock their potential. At the heart of these approaches is the principle of fostering autonomy while providing necessary support, ensuring that empowerment is a collaborative effort rather than a top-down imposition.

One of the most noteworthy strategies involves the integration of technology as a tool for empowerment. Digital platforms have democratized access to information and resources, enabling individuals to learn, connect, and innovate in unprecedented ways. Online learning platforms, for instance, provide opportunities for personal and professional development irrespective of geographical constraints. This not only enhances individual capabilities but also encourages a culture of continuous learning and adaptation, essential in today's rapidly evolving world.

Moreover, the rise of social media has transformed the landscape of community engagement and activism. These platforms serve as powerful catalysts for social change by amplifying voices that might otherwise remain unheard. They allow for the creation of virtual communities where ideas can be exchanged freely and collective action can be organized efficiently. This form of empowerment is particularly significant for marginalized groups, offering them a platform to challenge the status quo and advocate for their rights.

In the realm of organizational empowerment, a shift towards more participatory leadership styles is gaining traction. Leaders are increasingly embracing models that prioritize collaboration, inclusivity, and shared decision-making. By fostering an environment where team members feel valued and heard, organizations can harness a diverse range of insights and ideas. This leads to more innovative solutions and enhances employee satisfaction and retention.

Furthermore, the concept of design thinking is being adopted across various sectors to drive empowerment through creativity and empathy. This approach encourages problem-solving by deeply understanding the needs and challenges of those involved. By involving stakeholders in the design process, solutions are more likely to be effective and sustainable. Design thinking not only empowers individuals by allowing them to contribute actively to the development of solutions but also nurtures a mindset that values curiosity and experimentation.

Another innovative approach is the emphasis on mentorship and peer-to-peer learning. Building networks of support where individuals can share experiences and knowledge fosters a sense of community and mutual growth. Mentorship programs, both formal and informal, provide guidance and encouragement, helping individuals navigate challenges and seize opportunities. This relational dynamic is crucial for empowerment as it combines the benefits of personal experience with the wisdom of diverse perspectives.

Lastly, there is a growing recognition of the importance of mental and emotional well-being in the empowerment process. Initiatives that promote mindfulness, resilience, and emotional intelligence equip individuals with the skills to manage stress and adapt to change effectively. This holistic approach ensures that empowerment is not just about external achievements but also about internal growth and fulfillment.

Innovative approaches to empowerment are reshaping how we perceive and enact change. By leveraging technology, fostering inclusive leadership, embracing creative problem-solving, facilitating mentorship, and prioritizing well-being, we create environments where individuals and communities can flourish. These strategies underscore the importance of empowerment as an ongoing, dynamic process that nurtures potential and cultivates resilience in the face of ever-changing challenges.

Vision for an Empowered Society

Creating an inclusive setting is not only a moral issue but also a practical strategy that increases productivity, creativity, and well-being in any organization or society. Inclusion is about establishing the sense of belonging where everyone feels valued and respected regardless of background, ability, or opinion.

In the spirit of "Empower, Don't Overpower," inclusion is key to empowering people and groups to contribute their best to the organization. It involves acknowledging and appreciating diversity in all its dimensions, extending beyond the obvious aspects of race, gender, or age to include less visible dimensions such as thought diversity, education, and experience.

To really foster inclusion, it is first necessary to know and understand the barriers to complete participation of individuals. They can be systemic, i.e., policies or practices that inadvertently exclude certain people, or cultural, i.e., biases and stereotypes embedded in behavior and decision-making. To combat these barriers, one must take an active approach, starting with awareness and education. It is possible to train people on unconscious bias, cultural competence, and empathy, making them aware of their biases and at least trying to view the world from others' perspectives.

Communication is the core of inclusion building. Communication that is open and honest makes people feel free to express their ideas and experiences without fear of judgment or punishment. Providing space for this kind of communication in the form of regular meetings, forums, or social events is the core of trust and cohesion building among people in a community. Lastly, the provision of communication to everyone regardless of their language or ability is the basis of inclusive practice.

Leadership commitment is also a key element in building inclusion. Leaders set the tone for the organization or the community as a whole. Leaders practice inclusive behavior when they look for diverse input proactively and appreciate the inputs of all members. Leaders set the values of inclusion when they practice such behavior and get others to do so as well. Leaders must also commit to holding themselves and others accountable for building an inclusive environment, for example, in the speedy and effective resolution of acts of discrimination or exclusion.

Practices and policies must also be dedicated to inclusion and may include the allocation of flexible work arrangements to meet different needs, updating hiring and recruitment practices to ensure diversity, and developing clear respective behavior policies. Measuring and evaluating the effectiveness of inclusion efforts can also yield useful information and help to make improvements over time.

Building inclusion is an ongoing process that requires dedication and persistence from everyone involved. It is about building spaces where people can be themselves and where their diversity is not only tolerated but celebrated. By prioritizing inclusion, organizations and communities can unlock the potential of their members and gain higher innovation, resilience, and success.

In "Empower, Don't Overpower," the emphasis on inclusion is rooted in the belief that empowering others leads to bigger, more cohesive communities and organizations where everyone can thrive.

Epilogue

The Journey Forward

The process of empowerment is not a destination, it is a continual process of growth, trust, and transformation. At the end of this book, I want to reminded that leadership is not just about controlling, it's also about building confidence. We have learned throughout all the chapters that empowerment, established through empathy, communication, and vision, is a power that not only lifts individuals, but also reinforces institutions and communities.

This book was not just written as a guide but as a conversation, one that invites you to reflect, to act, and to grow. No matter if you are an organizational leader, a classroom teacher, a parent in your household, or a dedicated citizen in your community, you possess the power to empower. It is in the choices we make every day, in the trust we place, and in the space, we create for others to fly, that real transformation starts to set in.

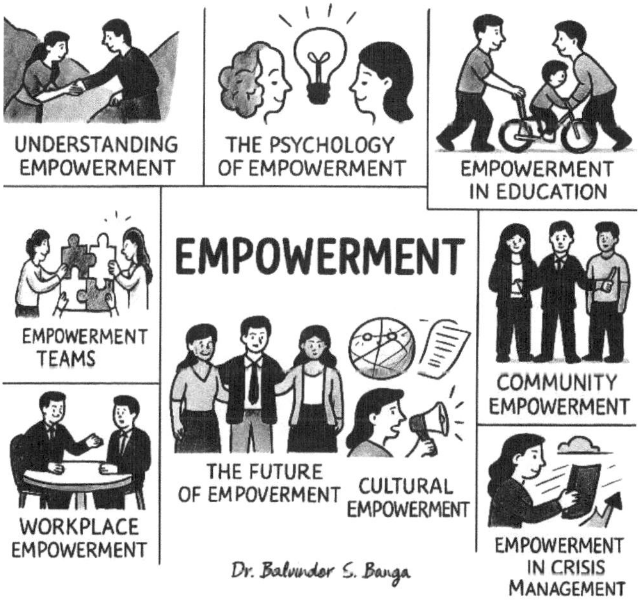

As you leave these pages behind, take with you not only the learning and the approaches, but the spirit of high-trust leadership. Make "**Empower, Don't Overpower**" a call to action one that resounds in boardrooms and classrooms, around dinner plates and on the web. Let us create a future together where empowerment is the norm, not the exception…

— Dr. Balvinder S. Banga